WHAT WORKS
WHEN LIFE DOESN'T

STUART BRISCOE was born in Millom, Cumbria, England, where he embarked on a career in banking and preaching at the age of seventeen. In 1970 Stuart became pastor of Elmbrook Church in Brookfield, Wisconsin. He has authored more than forty books, preached in more than one hundred countries, and is invited to minister to pastors, missionaries, and church lay-leaders on all continents. Stuart and his wife, Jill, are now ministers-at-large at Elmbrook. They have three children and thirteen grandchildren.

WHAT WORKS
WHEN LIFE DOESN'T

WHAT GOD HAS TO SAY ABOUT LIFE'S DIFFICULTIES AND HOW TO HANDLE THEM

STUART BRISCOE

HOWARD
PUBLISHING CO.

Our purpose at Howard Publishing is to:

• *Increase faith* in the hearts of growing Christians

• *Inspire holiness* in the lives of believers

• *Instill hope* in the hearts of struggling people everywhere

Because He's coming again!

WHAT WORKS WHEN LIFE DOESN'T © 2004 by Stuart Briscoe

All rights reserved. Printed in the United States of America

Published by Howard Publishing Co., Inc.
3117 North 7th Street, West Monroe, LA 71291-2227
www.howardpublishing.com
In association with the literary agency of Alive Communications, Inc.
7680 Goddard Street, Suite 200 Colorado Springs, CO 80920

04 05 06 07 08 09 10 11 12 13   10 9 8 7 6 5 4 3 2

Cover design by David Carlson Design
Interior design by Gabe Cardinale

Briscoe, D. Stuart.
    What works when life doesn't : what God has to say about life's difficulties and how to handle them / Stuart Briscoe.
        p. cm.
    ISBN 1-58229-374-0
    1. Bible. O.T. Psalms—Sermons. 2. Sermons, American. I. Title.

BS1430.54.B75 2004
248.8—dc22

2004054265

Scriptures not otherwise marked are taken from the HOLY BIBLE, NEW INTERNATIONAL VERSION®. Copyright © 1973, 1978, 1984 by International Bible Society. Used by permission of Zondervan Publishing House. Scriptures marked NKJV are taken from The New King James Version/Thomas Nelson Publishers, Nashville: Thomas Nelson Publishers. Copyright © 1982. Used by permission. All rights reserved. Scriptures marked NLT are taken from the Holy Bible, New Living Translation, copyright © 1996. Used by permission of Tyndale House Publishers, Inc., Wheaton, Illinois 60189. All rights reserved. Scriptures marked KJV are taken from The Holy Bible, Authorized King James Version, © 1961 by The National Publishing Co. Scriptures marked NASB are taken from the NEW AMERICAN STANDARD BIBLE®, Copyright © 1960, 1962, 1963, 1968, 1971, 1972, 1973, 1975, 1977, 1995 by The Lockman Foundation. Used by permission.

To Mary,
my mother,
who brought me to life,
who led me to Christ,
who taught me to work,
who inspired me to preach,
and who, during the preparation of this manuscript,
battled cancer with quiet courage and unshaken faith,
proving once again that she knows
"what works when life doesn't."

CONTENTS

For many years I regarded the psalms almost as optional extras to "mainline spiritual truth"—the sort of thing you read when you are too sick to concentrate or too tired to keep awake for more than a few minutes. I enjoyed singing them with Presbyterians, chanting them with Episcopalians, quoting them to the dying, and reading them in my devotions. But they were little more than the frosting on the cake—the work of mystical poets mixed in with the "important" work of realistic theologians to make it a little more palatable.

My problem was that though I had read, sung, chanted, and warbled the psalms, I had never really studied them. When I did, I had a big surprise!

I became so excited with my study that I embarked on a yearlong series of sermons to the congregation of Elmbrook Church. I taught on the psalms as I spoke to missionaries in foreign countries, students in academic settings, and to businesspeople. I preached the psalms on radio broadcasts. I talked about them to anybody who would listen. And do you know what I discovered? Just about everyone expressed the same surprise I had felt:

"I never realized how clearly the psalms speak to the pertinent issues of our day."

"We had read the psalms before going to sleep at night, but we never studied them as God's Word to us for day-to-day activities."

"We didn't realize the clarity of the world-view expressed in this part of the Bible."

Now, many years later, I'm still finding that people in all sorts of situations are interested to know what God has to say through the psalms. They touch on real-life issues and provide a view of a very personal God—a reality we urgently need in today's impersonal and complex world. May these studies continue to show many people what will work when their lives don't.

ACKNOWLEDGMENTS

Naturally, I have being greatly helped in my personal study of the psalms by the work of numerous authors, none of whom surpass the value to me of my fellow Brit, Charles Haddon Spurgeon. His The Treasury of David, while dated, is still deeply enriching and unmistakably relevant.

As always I am grateful for the attention to detail and quiet efficiency of my agent, Andrea Christian, of Alive Publications. And I gladly welcome this, my first opportunity to find out firsthand that the Howard Publishing people are great people to work with.

Psalm 1

*1 Blessed is the man
who does not walk in the counsel of the wicked
or stand in the way of sinners
or sit in the seat of mockers.
2 But his delight is in the law of the LORD,
and on his law he meditates day and night.
3 He is like a tree planted by streams of water,
which yields its fruit in season
and whose leaf does not wither.
Whatever he does prospers.*

*4 Not so the wicked!
They are like chaff
that the wind blows away.
5 Therefore the wicked will not stand in the judgment,
nor sinners in the assembly of the righteous.*

*6 For the LORD watches over the way of the righteous,
but the way of the wicked will perish.*

CHAPTER ONE

WHEN HAPPINESS
ELUDES YOU

When an elderly American lady asked me whether we have a Fourth of July in England, my immediate response was, "No ma'am, we go straight from the third to the fifth!"

I learned my history in England, and when I came to the United States, I knew so little about the events of 1776 that I wouldn't have recognized a Declaration of Independence if I'd tripped over it. But times have definitely changed. Now I know that the Declaration of Independence says that we have three inalienable rights: "life, liberty, and the pursuit of happiness." But I have often wondered why there are so many unhappy people in a country where freedom to pursue happiness is one of the most cherished rights.

WHAT IS HAPPINESS ANYWAY?
"Blessed is the man . . ." (v. 1a)

One reason so many people are unhappy is that, though they are busy pursuing happiness, they aren't all that sure what happiness is. People want to be happy, but most of those I talk with seem to think that happiness will come

1

their way when everything else starts to go their way. It's the happiness that says, like the old song from Oklahoma, "I've got a wonderful feeling, everything's going my way." But life isn't like that, except in musicals. We simply cannot expect everything to always go our way. If our happiness is dependent on life turning out the way we expect it, then I'm afraid we're in for a fair measure of unhappiness.

The Bible shows, however, that happiness is not necessarily related to what happens to us, and that it is possible to be happy in difficult and unpleasant circumstances. The apostle Paul talked a lot about joy when he was in prison. The Lord Jesus told his disciples to "rejoice and be glad" when they were persecuted because they belonged to him (Matthew 5:12). So it is obvious that happiness and joy are more than good feelings resulting from pleasant circumstances.

The Greeks were of the opinion that their gods were having a great time. They used the word makarios ("blessed") to describe it, which means to be "enriched, contented, and fulfilled."

This word appears in the New Testament in such verses as "Blessed are the poor in spirit" (Matthew 5:3). The Greek translation of Psalm 1 uses the same word: "Blessed is the man who does not walk in the counsel of the wicked or stand in the way of sinners or sit in the seat of mockers" (v. 1).

WHERE IS HAPPINESS FOUND?

"... who does not walk ..." (v. 1b)

The psalmist makes it quite clear that we will not find happiness in certain places. That gives us another clue as to why many people aren't finding happiness. They don't know where to seek it. People who are free to pursue happiness will not find it if they don't know what it is, or if they chase after it where it isn't.

It was January 1, 1964, when I arrived on my first visit to the United States. I turned on the television and saw a picture the like of which I had never seen before. It was a rearview shot of a row of big men in tight pants bending over in such a way that they appeared to be putting intolerable strain on their pants. Behind them stood a man who seemed to have lost his temper completely. He was yelling and shouting, apparently because the other men had his ball and he wanted it back. Eventually, after much shouting, they gave it to him. He promptly gave it to one of his friends, who ran a few steps, then received an awful beating by some other men wearing similar tight pants, but of a different color.

They were apparently very sorry about their behavior because, after they had beaten him up, they gathered in a small group to pray about it. They were not sincere, however, because they went straight back and did the same thing again.

After repeating this whole outrageous procedure about ten times, the man with the ball suddenly threw it about sixty yards to another man I hadn't noticed before. He caught it, ran a few yards, did a funny little dance, and the crowd went wild. I thought I had stumbled onto some religious festival (subsequently I discovered I was right!) and was completely mystified until someone started to explain what was happening so that a newly arrived Englishman could understand.

Apparently, the quarterback had so effectively faked a hand-off to his running back that the defensive line and linebackers had played the run, leaving the receiver wide open to catch the pass and go in for a touchdown. And it all happened because the defensive players chased the man without the ball.

The moral of the story is, if you are free to pursue happiness, don't be faked into pursuing it where it isn't!

UNGODLY COUNSEL

". . . in the counsel of the wicked . . ." (v. 1b)

The King James Version of the Bible expresses it "the counsel of the ungodly." Happiness can never be found in a lifestyle that leaves God out of the picture. Atheists choose to believe that God does not exist. They do this by faith, quite obviously, because they have no concrete evidence that there is no God. But atheists have a major problem: if there is no God behind the universe, then there is no reason behind their own existence. Both they and their world are the result of fate, the chance products of meaningless events.

"Are you alive?" I asked a teenager in a coffeehouse one evening.

"Yes," he said, looking startled.

"Why are you alive?" I asked next.

"Because I was born and haven't died."

"Did you have anything to do with your birth?"

"No, except I was there!"

"Do you plan on having anything to do with your death?"

"No."

"Then as far as you are concerned, your birth was an accident and your death will be an accident."

"I suppose you're right."

"Then I know what you are. You are an accident suspended between two accidents."

He looked thoughtful for a moment and said, "You know something—that helps me understand myself better than anything I've heard."

Many people do not believe there is a God behind their birth, who has a plan for their life and who wants to one day take them to be with him for all eternity. They are therefore faced with the unpleasant prospect of having no real purpose for their existence. They must either sink into despair as a result, or do anything that will help them to stop thinking seriously.

A godless philosophy produces some people who give up on life and others who try to keep themselves going by filling their nagging emptiness with banal trivialities. Either way, those people never feel fulfilled. It's difficult to believe you are a meaningless accident and to feel good about it!

"The counsel of the wicked" or the "ungodly" does not refer only to the philosophies of atheists, however. It can also describe the way of life adopted by people who give lip service to God but don't feel it necessary to actually regard him as God. The whole concept of God assumes that he is supreme, that "he's the greatest." But it is too easy to say you believe in the Supreme One and yet refuse to give him the supreme place in your life. This approach to life is little more than atheism with an ecclesiastical facade.

You can be an atheist, a Baptist, a Methodist, an Adventist, or any other "ist" and still live according to the "counsel of the ungodly." There can be a serious conflict between your knowledge of God's requirements and your degree of willingness to obey him. Tension results and severe unhappiness and discontent inevitably follow. There's no happiness in a godless philosophy, however you look at it.

MISSING THE STANDARD

". . . or stand in the way of sinners . . ." (v. 1c)

As we have seen, happiness is not to be found "in the counsel of the wicked." Nor is it to be found *"in the way of sinners."* Most people seem to think that a sinner is someone who does what they don't do! This position may seem comfortable for some, but it is false—like a first-class seat on the wrong plane. From the biblical perspective, a sinner is a person who "misses the target," so far as achievement is concerned, or one who misses the point, so far as truth is concerned. So a sinner has severe problems.

God has given people a target to aim for, and they keep missing it. Many people know they are failing, and in all sincerity they keep trying and missing. This is terribly frustrating for them. They feel guilty and helpless and decidedly unhappy.

But there are many others who simply are not aware of God's standards, so they are not even aware that they are missing them. In fact, they don't know what they're supposed to be hitting. This reminds me of an experience in my marine training. We were taken to the firing range in the middle of the night and told to engage in "night firing." The main problem we encountered was that we couldn't see any targets. What an exercise in futility!

People who do not have God at the base of their thinking will have no guidelines at the root of their behaving. And that is as unfulfilling as it is frustrating.

MOCKERS AND CYNICS

". . . or sit in the seat of mockers." (v. 1d)

If you walk long enough and then stand around for a while, you will soon need a comfortable seat. Look where the person who walks in the counsel of the wicked and stands in the way of sinners finds himself: *"in the seat of mockers."*

This comes as no surprise. Godless philosophy leads to a sense of purposelessness and a lifestyle that is frustrating, but there is a limit to the purposelessness and frustration that most people can take. Sooner or later they give up and become hard-boiled cynics. They mock any suggestion that God is real, they mock any standards that purport to come from God, and they minimize the efforts of God's people to bring a message of hope to the hopeless and comfort to the troubled.

We live in a cynical age. People are cynical concerning most institutions, many politicians, and much theology. They laugh at absolute moral standards and attack divine principles. But they put little of value in the vacuum they create, and their cynicism not only leads to increased societal anguish—it rarely brings much joy to the cynics themselves.

DELIGHTING IN THE WORD

"But his delight is in the law of the LORD, and on his law he meditates day and night." (v. 2)

The word *but* is a key word in Bible study, for it alerts the reader to the fact that there is another side to what has been said, and this alternative viewpoint is about to be presented. So far the psalmist has taken great pains to state where happiness is not. Now he speaks positively about the direction in which happiness can be sought and found. *"But his delight is in the law of the LORD"* gives the clue that so many people need to discover.

The phrase "Happiness is . . ." could bring to mind a rubber duck, a benign tumor, or assorted other things and experiences. But the happiness we are talking about is found only in a relationship with the Lord. Just as godless philosophy is doomed to disappointment, the opposite view leads to the opposite experience. Instead of taking a leap of faith and deciding that God isn't, we must take the leap of faith and believe that he is.

The Bible makes no attempt to prove that God is. It simply starts by saying "In the beginning God" (Genesis 1:1), and then develops that theme throughout the Bible's sixty-six books. The evidence for reasonable faith that God does exist is piled high for all but the totally obdurate to believe.

But having said that happiness is to be found in believing that God is, we must add that the God of whom we speak is not a vague force or a creative influence, but one who speaks to us through his Word.

The *"law of the LORD"* refers to God's requirements for humanity—what people should do and what they should not do. It stipulates what will happen if they do and what they can expect if they don't.

Imagine what it would be like if you had to earn your living by playing football, but the game in which you played had no ball, no goals, no sidelines, no yard marks, no rules, no scores, no officials, no spectators, no end, and no result. Day after day, you would have to play a game of meaningless nonsense, dragging yourself out of bed morning by morning, steeling yourself for another day of unmitigated nothingness.

Now think of the difference that rules and goals and officials and results make. Godless philosophy wants you to play a game without rules, but the law of the Lord ensures a meaningful game based on meaningful rules. There is no comparison.

Of course you have to know the rules, and that is why the fulfilled person not only knows that the Lord has spoken, but delights in what he has said and makes every effort to learn and follow God's instructions.

It is one thing to *meditate day and night,*" but it's another thing to play according to the rules. This is where we tend to come unglued. No person alive has fully followed through on all of God's requirements. But even here there is more opportunity to be joyful: those who acknowledge their sin and seek the Lord can experience total forgiveness, because Christ died that we might be forgiven. You can't find happier people than those who know what they should be and know they haven't been that, but who have confessed their faults and failures and have been forgiven. "Oh, what joy for those whose disobedience is forgiven, whose sins are put out of sight. Yes, what joy for those whose sin is no longer counted against them by the Lord" (Romans 4:7–8 NLT).

After the Lord has done his great forgiving work, he sends the Holy Spirit to live in the forgiven sinner. The Holy Spirit is the one who inspired the law of the Lord in the first place, and when he comes into a person's life, he begins to impart to that person the power to obey God's law. Paul said, "The requirement of the law [is] fully accomplished for us who no longer follow our sinful nature but instead follow the Spirit" (Romans 8:4 NLT).

There is something very attractive and distinctive about such a life, particularly when it is contrasted with so many of the hard, harsh, cynical, unhappy lives produced by those who sit in the seat of the scornful.

A STURDY TREE

"He is like a tree planted by streams of water . . ." (v. 3a)

The psalm moves into a description of the fulfilled life with the words of this verse.

I've always loved trees, possibly because I spent my early boyhood in the Lake District of England. Beside the lakes and rivers the trees are tall and straight, but up in the mountains many trees are scrawny and appear to be hanging on the sides of precipices, solely concerned with survival. The difference, of course, is that the majestic trees draw nourishment from the water in the lakes and streams.

People are like that for the same reason. If people don't have their roots deep into the river of God, they are fully occupied trying to cope with the chill winds and raging storms of their unfortunate circumstances. But those same storms and winds fail to ruffle the composure or threaten the stability of the person planted by the river. There are some people whose lives under strain are so unusual that others are amazed at the strength they exhibit and the sense of deep joy they exude. And it is all attributable to the work of the Spirit of God.

PRODUCING FRUIT IN SEASON

". . . which yields its fruit in season . . ." (v. 3b)

Trees and people are expected to do more that just stand around looking tall and straight. They are supposed to produce fruit. In fact, there is no way that a totally unproductive person can be fulfilled or happy. Many have tried to be happy and lazy, but they have failed, because God made human beings to be productive.

Several years ago I appeared on a television show dealing with the subject of work. A young woman wrote in:

> I work in a gas station, and I don't always feel like getting up at 5:00 a.m. 'cause it's still dark outside, but once I get some cereal in my stomach and get going, I'm okay. I may not have the most beautiful job in the world, but I'm doing a service for other people for the glory of God. If I would go to work with a crummy attitude and would be mean and crabby to all my customers, they would go to their jobs and families and be crabby, too. Just think of all the people this would affect. There would be one bad chain reaction. But I pray that each day I will give good service and a friendly smile to all of the customers who come my way.

How would you like to work at a gas station at five o'clock in the morning during a Wisconsin winter? Do you think you could be happy? You could be, if you were convinced that God had put you there "like a tree planted by the river."

You would also be able to bring forth your *"fruit in season."* Fruit is the external evidence of your internal life. Oranges growing on branches lead one to assume that the branches belong to an orange tree. People rooted in the Spirit of God work in the power of the Spirit, and the fruit shows in their work and in their attitudes. Love, joy, and peace begin to sprout all over the place. It's the happy life.

LEAVES THAT DON'T WITHER

". . . and whose leaf does not wither." (v. 3c)

Trees look great in the fall, so long as you don't look too closely. But if you do happen to get too close, you will find that the glorious colors are actually the colors of death. The once fresh, green leaves are heading for the ground, soon to drive people into a frenzy of raking and burning. It's a pity it has to be like that, because some trees don't behave that way. They are evergreens. They don't start with fragrant freshness in the spring, curl up in the heat of summer, and fall in autumn to be covered by the snows of winter. They keep going. Their *"leaf does not wither."* They exhibit consistency and quiet determination.

Our Lord Jesus was a beautiful example of not withering. When Peter "advised" him not to go to Jerusalem, Jesus made it abundantly clear that he was going. When he got to Jerusalem, he quietly and methodically put his affairs in order. He gave final instructions to his disciples, prayed about their situation, talked with the Father, and kept moving relentlessly toward his goal. Pilate with all his persuasion couldn't move him. Herod couldn't get anywhere with him. Even the mob in the garden seemed to come under his authority.

Even on the cross, Jesus didn't wither in his determination to fulfill all that had been spoken of him. He refused the anesthetic offered to him, dealt with the needs of his mother, and even prayed for his enemies. When he was through, he still didn't wither. When all was finished, he gave up his spirit to his Father with a great shout.

Most of us probably couldn't imagine ourselves either living or dying with anything approaching our Lord's level of determination, but we can live a whole lot nearer to his example than we usually do. The same Holy Spirit through whom Christ offered himself to God is the river of our resource to make us like evergreen trees, whose leaves never wither.

TRUE PROSPERITY

"Whatever he does prospers." (v. 3d)

These words must surely be one of the most fascinating promises in Scripture. We tend to equate prosperity with wealth, and wealth with money. Many people take this promise as a divine guarantee that if they do things God's way, they will make their fortune. In fact, it is not uncommon to hear businessmen attribute their wealth to their godliness. This kind of thinking must be treated with care, because the Bible points out that the "love of money is the root of all kinds of evil" (1 Timothy 6:10). For some people, more money would mean more temptation than they could handle—which would lead to disaster, not prosperity.

God is promising prosperity of life rather than of bank accounts. He is assuring those who obey him and honor him that in their obedience and trust they will find enrichment of life. This will mean far more to their true happiness than any amount of material prosperity.

Joseph was sold as a slave, but as a slave he honored God and God prospered him. God didn't set Joseph free at once, and Joseph didn't make a personal fortune, but he changed the course of a nation and altered human history. Through Joseph's servitude in Egypt, God was able to get the Israelites into Egypt and later into the Promised Land.

I once counseled a couple who had gone through deep water since committing their lives to Christ. They had been sincere in their commitment and careful in their discipleship, but it hadn't led to material prosperity. Illness had not been banished from their experience. Persecution had come their way in the loss of a job. Nevertheless, they have *prospered* through it all. As people, they became deeper, more contented, and better able to cope with life. They came to see that God was truly prospering them in the way that he wanted them to go.

A WORD OF WARNING TO THE WICKED

"Not so the wicked! They are like chaff that the wind blows away. Therefore the wicked will not stand in the judgment, nor sinners in the assembly of the righteous. . . . But the way of the wicked will perish." (vv. 4–6)

The psalmist sounds a somber note as well as a happy one: there is a chill about those words *"not so."* All the majestic themes that have been applied to the life of believers are shown to be irrelevant to unbelievers. Unbelievers will hear all that applies to them. They must understand that their lives will be as empty as the *"chaff that the wind blows away."* They *"will not stand in the judgment."* (They *will* have to appear before God in judgment, but when they do so, they won't have a leg to stand on!) And they most assuredly will not be *"in the assembly of the righteous."*

In short, *"the way of the wicked will perish."* The joy of believers is always tinged with pain, for while they enjoy the riches of forgiveness and the resources of the Spirit, they are surrounded by those who are impoverished in soul and defeated in spirit. While they live a fruitful, consistent life, they encounter daily those who are disenchanted and discouraged. But Christians do not ignore or dismiss the ungodly; rather, for Christ's sake, they love them and endeavor to share with them the alternatives God offers. The rich man in Christ's story lived in luxury while Lazarus was dying miserably (see Luke 16:19–31).

Not so the happy person. The happy person shares his or her joy and reaches out to those who are perishing.

THE LORD KNOWS ALL

"For the LORD watches over the way of the righteous . . ."
(v. 6a)

Above and beyond everything else, the believer has the calm, settled assurance that all is well and that God is honoring these who honor him. This assurance is more conducive to real happiness than we can imagine. But to realize that God "watches over the way of the righteous," which leads to heaven ("the assembly of the righteous"), is even more thrilling. It means that God is in control of every situation into which his obedient child moves and that every step of the way is leading ultimately to glory.

Psalm 2

[1] Why do the nations conspire
and the peoples plot in vain?
[2] The kings of the earth take their stand
and the rulers gather together
against the LORD
and against his Anointed One.
[3] "Let us break their chains," they say,
"and throw off their fetters."

[4] The One enthroned in heaven laughs;
the Lord scoffs at them.
[5] Then he rebukes them in his anger
and terrifies them with his wrath, saying,
[6] "I have installed my King
on Zion, my holy hill."

[7] I will proclaim the decree of the Lord:

He said to me, "You are my Son;
today I have become your Father.
[8] Ask of me,
and I make the nations in your inheritance,
the ends of the earth your possession.
[9] You will rule them with an iron scepter;
you will dash them to pieces like pottery."

[10] Therefore, you kings, be wise;
be warned, you rulers of the earth.
[11] Serve the LORD with fear
and rejoice with trembling.
[12] Kiss the Son, lest he be angry
and you be destroyed in your way,
for his wrath can flare up in a moment.
Blessed are all who take refuge in him.

WHEN THE WORLD IS FALLING APART

There was a time when believers who asked questions about their faith were treated with suspicion. The inference was that they wouldn't need to ask questions if they really believed. Today, it is now permissible to have an inquiring mind, so, hopefully, more people with a more intelligent faith will have a greater impact on our world.

However, many believers still do not ask enough questions. Perhaps they just aren't interested enough to think through the tenets of their faith. Or perhaps they are so insecure in the Lord that any difficulty puts intolerable strain on their life.

Whatever the case may be, there is no doubt that the person who wrote this psalm felt free to question many things going on in his world. He asked two big questions that needed to be asked—questions that need to be answered today, as in every generation.

WHY, GOD?

"Why do the nations conspire and the peoples plot in vain?" (v. 1)

The first question was *"Why do the nations conspire?"* The meaning of the Hebrew in contemporary terms would be "Why is there so much international conflict?" Every thinking person in our world ought to be asking the same question. Unrest and bloodshed are happening in every corner of our world. The horror of war has become so commonplace now that we can sit at home eating supper while watching the latest carnage graphically portrayed on our television screens.

How many of us are asking the hard questions: What is the cause of all this senseless belligerence? Why is the Middle East constantly embroiled in conflict? Can peace ever come to Iraq or to Afghanistan? Why are so many of the nations formerly a part of the Soviet Union now seeing the rebirth of ancient ethnic conflicts? Will it ever end? Is there any hope?

The second question carries the same weight of concern as the first: *"Why do the peoples plot in vain?"* The word *vain* in the Bible conveys the idea of emptiness, futility, and confusion. The question really is, "Why is there so much individual confusion?"

- Why do so many people carefully study their horoscopes or call psychic lines, when it is obvious that horoscopes and psychics are 90 percent nonsense and 10 percent worse than nonsense?
- Why are so many people attracted to Eastern mysticism and various New Age religious movements?

- Why are desperate marriage partners chasing after a new cure for a wedlock that had degenerated into deadlock?
- Why do people still pursue extramarital relationships despite the well-known evidence of the social and even health-related risks of such behavior?

Spiritual, social, and philosophical confusion abounds in our postmodern culture, and unfortunately it shows no sign of abating. The danger is that believers might adopt an attitude of calculated indifference to the problems surrounding them. They may feel that they are all right personally, and unable to change the behavior of other people. This indifference would be understandable if there were no answers, but since there are sound biblical answers available for any problem a believer encounters, it is totally inexcusable.

KINGS AND RULERS ON TALK SHOWS

"The kings of the earth take their stand and the rulers gather together . . ." (v. 2a–b)

In true rhetorical fashion the psalmist answers his own questions before anyone can get a word in! When this psalm was written, kings and rulers had the power to exert great influence on their subjects and were able to lead them for good or evil in whatever direction they chose. Today we have national leaders and charismatic personalities who are able to persuade and influence far more people than did the kings and rulers of ancient times. The mass media have had an unparalleled influence on our contemporary society, not to mention the astonishing impact the Internet has had on the entire world with its instant dispersion of information. Talk-show hosts can sell their philosophies of life to millions without moving from their ornate sets. Web sites can post their worldviews for the entire world to peruse. The celebrity guests on talk shows, who start in the seat of honor and slowly slide to oblivion off the end of the couch, are able to influence thousands of marriages by sharing their personal experiences. Often, unfortunately, their chief "qualification" for such monumental exposure may be an ability to outstrip a defensive secondary or to win a key political primary.

The *"kings and rulers"* of our day do not sit on thrones or lead their people into battle. Many of them sit in Madison Avenue offices dispensing their philosophy of life in million-dollar advertising campaigns. They work feverishly in recording studios in Nashville, turning out CDs whose lyrics will shape the thinking of millions. Or from their luxurious penthouses they plan the articles that will hit the newsstands in slick, sophisticated formats.

There is, of course, the possibility that men and women of real spiritual caliber may take places of influence and lead people in the paths of righteousness. But it is more possibility than probability. It just isn't happening to any marked degree.

AGAINST GOD

" . . . against the LORD . . ." (v. 2c)

Whoever today's *"kings"* are and wherever they meet, most of them have one thing in common: they *"gather together against the LORD."* That is to say, their whole approach to life and, accordingly, the influence they exert on society are contrary to the Lord's righteous ways. They gather themselves together and leave God out of the picture. What they have to offer society is the product of their own worldly thinking. Unfortunately, as a society we hear the voice of fallible humans more than the infallible God, whose wisdom has no limits. We are drinking in more human error than eternal truth. We learn to adore human personalities, not God, and to worship success rather than the Lord, the Creator of all.

The psalmist had no doubt that the leaders of his day were *"against the LORD."* Their hostility to the Lord was open and without embarrassment. They saw no reason to hide it, and they didn't try to. It is important that we should understand this hostility, because the situation is the same today as it was back then.

When LORD appears in small capital letters in the Bible, it signifies the name of Israel's God, sometimes transliterated as either "Jehovah" or "Yahweh." This name, regarded by the Jews as too sacred to fall from their lips or even to flow from their pens, is obscure in its origin, but we do know that it has to do with God's eternal, unique being. God described himself as "I AM WHO I AM" (Exodus 3:14). "I will be what I will be" is perhaps a more accurate rendering of the Hebrew.

Either way, the name of Jehovah conveys a great sense of independence, self-sufficiency, and determination. It suggests, "I am what I am, I'll do what I'll do, and I'll accomplish what I please!" It gives warning to us humans that we had better not confuse God with anyone else, or try to take God's rightful place.

It should be obvious that the very idea of a self-existent, self-sufficient, totally unique God does not appeal to people who would use the same words to describe themselves! Self-sufficient men and women don't want to hear about self-existent Jehovah. Self-determined men and women have nothing but hatred for a message that is based on the statement that God is the one who determines. Arrogant leaders will always resist acknowledging God's existence and power and glory.

AGAINST THE ANOINTED ONE

". . . and against his Anointed One." (v. 2d)

The title *Christ*, given to the Lord Jesus, is closely related to the Greek word *Christos*, which means *"Anointed One."* In fact, Psalm 2:1–2 was quoted by the early disciples in the prayer recorded in Acts 4:25–26. The Anointed One of this psalm becomes the Lord Jesus himself in that prayer. It is not surprising, then, that in our world there is not only hostility to the very idea of Jehovah but also great resistance to the biblical message of Christ.

In Old Testament times, people were anointed as prophets, priests, or kings to show that they had God's approval and were acting as agents on his behalf. Jesus Christ came as God's agent par excellence. He would reign over more people than any king, reveal more truth than any prophet, and lead more sinners to reconciliation than any priest. In short, he came to do for us what we could not do for ourselves. He came to redeem us from sin. Self-sufficient men and women, wrapped up in their own schemes, content with their sins, and bent on living their own lives don't want to know about a Redeemer. The last thing they want to hear is that a Savior has come. They look for answers down here, so they have no time for a Christ who came as the answer from "up there."

Painful as it is for believers to realize, we live in a world that is basically opposed to God's revelation that he is Jehovah and that his Son is Lord of all. For contemporary society to admit these two things would mean a complete reversal of its thinking and a total revolution in lifestyle.

CHAINS AND FETTERS

"'Let us break their chains,' they say, 'and throw off their fetters.'" (v. 3)

Human leaders are extremely vocal. Opinion makers are busy making opinions and selling them attractively pack-aged. And listen to what they are saying: "*'Let us break their chains,' they say, 'and throw off their fetters.'*" Yet, the chains and fetters that they wish to rid themselves of are the righteous principles and standards of Jehovah and his Christ.

Much contemporary philosophy is as old as David's era. In fact, it's older. It's as old as Adam. Adam decided to get rid of his "chains and fetters," anticipating that he would be enriched as a result. He got that bright idea from Lucifer. Lucifer was once a beautiful angel who had a superb position in the heavenlies, but it greatly angered him that he wasn't "the Most High" (see Isaiah 14:14). To be restricted in this area of his experience was more than he was prepared to tolerate, so he decided to break the chains and fetters and be as God.

Today, some psychologists and other cultural spokespersons tell us that Christian morality is outdated and that Christian principles are repressive. The advice they give in exchange for their fat fees is, "Let us break their chains and fetters." Various so-called liberation movements are taking careful aim at all "repressive" institutions, and many of them say that Public Enemy Number One is the church.

Many young people have chafed at the parental controls that have been placed upon them. Due to the prevailing economic climate, they have often been able to leave home and head out on their own. Their quest, of course, is the same as the quest of Lucifer, of Adam, of the kings and rulers of Psalm 2, and of the opinion makers, frustrated husbands and wives, and assorted other rebels of our own day. They look for the freedom they believe God has denied them by his "repressive" requirements. They believe that if they can only rid themselves of the "chains and fetters," their new freedom will fill their lives with peace and joy and love.

Instead, anarchy and chaos increase, and growing numbers of desperate people look for answers that are not forthcoming from the misguided leaders they have followed. The scene is more bleak today than when Psalm 2 was penned.

MUD OR STARS

"The One enthroned in heaven . . ." (v. 4a)

It was Frederick Langbridge who said, "Two men look out through the same bars; / One sees the mud and one sees the stars." He was referring to perspective, of course. Downcast looks guarantee a view of mud. It takes an upward look to see the stars. Having done plenty of mud-watching, the psalmist suddenly takes to stargazing. What a delightful and refreshing relief! After the heavy question, the depressing evaluation, the sense of foreboding and hopelessness, he lifts up his eyes and reminds us that there is another perspective for this fallen world—the perspective of heaven. He turns our attention to "the One enthroned in heaven."

How easy it is to forget God in our fast-paced world! How prone even believers become to seeing only the horrors of their world. Some close their eyes and hope the horrors will all go away. Others commit themselves to lives of sacrifice and service, endeavoring to stem the corruption and ease the pain. But whatever else happens, God must not be overlooked because he sits *"in heaven."* This expression gives a great picture of God's majestic throne, far above "the restless world that wars below." It adds a dimension to human existence without which despair is the only option.

IS GOD LAUGHING AND SCOFFING?

"[The Lord] laughs; the LORD scoffs at them." (v. 4a–b)

But what is God doing in heaven? Why is he not intervening in the troubles that plague our world? The answer that the psalmist gives to those questions serves mainly to raise more questions: *"The One enthroned in heaven laughs"*! Does that mean God derives great amusement from the pitiful children in developing nations who have known nothing but poverty and war all their short lives? Does it mean he gets slightly hysterical about bloodshed and anguish?

No! God's laughter is not from amusement or hysteria; it is the laughter of "scoffing" or derision. God has never heard anything so ludicrous as the empty boastings of these human beings who are rebelling against him. To his ears there is nothing more ridiculous than the arrogant rhetoric of a fallen humanity that has repeatedly proved itself incompetent to manage its own affairs. He totally rejects any suggestions from proud humans that their conflict and confusion can be resolved without reference to him. He has no time at all for ingenious schemes that ignore his sovereignty and replace it with the sovereignty of created beings. The Creator refuses to bow to the creature. He insists on the converse. The creature must acknowledge him as Lord, and only then will peace reign in the world.

IS GOD ANGRY?

"Then he rebukes them in his anger and
terrifies them in his wrath . . ." (v. 5)

We have a hard time grasping the incommunicable attributes of God. Our problem is that we have only human attributes as comparisons. When we consider the love of God, we tend to think of the most loving father or mother we ever knew and attribute his or her characteristics to God. This comparison, no doubt, helps in our understanding of God; but how are we to understand God's wrath and displeasure? Do we think of the angriest parent we have ever encountered?

Does God raise his voice, get red in the face, allow his own feelings to cloud his objectivity, and sometimes lose control?

The wrath of God is as pure as the holiness of God. It is as consistent with his being as is his love. When God is angry, he is perfectly angry. When he is displeased about something, there is every reason that he should be—if he were not displeased in that circumstance, he would be less than perfect. His wrath and his displeasure are absolute necessities to his divine moral perfection.

We tend to think of anger as sin. But sometimes it is sinful not to be angry. If I do something wrong and am accused of the wrongdoing, I may become very angry. That anger would be simply adding sin to sin. But if I see someone being abused and maltreated, and instead of going to that person's aid I walk away, then my lack of anger is sin.

It is unthinkable that God would not be purely and perfectly angry with sin. If he failed to deal judiciously with sin in righteous anger, we could never again be sure that wrong will ultimately be punished and right rewarded. And if we stop believing that, we immediately become dyed-in-the-wool cynics.

GOD ON THE THRONE

"I have installed my King on Zion, my holy hill. I will proclaim the decree of the LORD: He said to me, 'You are my Son; today I have become your Father. Ask of me, and I will make the nations your inheritance, the ends of the earth your possession. You will rule them with an iron scepter; you will dash them to pieces like pottery.'" (vv. 6–9)

Fortunately, God does not just sit on his throne seething in silence. He speaks of setting up a king on his *"holy hill."* The wording of the King James Version shows a stark contrast at this point: In verse 2 it reads, "The kings of the earth set themselves," then here, *"I have installed my king."* In the New Testament, passages such as Acts 13 and Hebrews 1 identify this king as the risen, ascended Lord Jesus Christ.

The risen Lord now speaks with calm authority, outlining his status, his expectations, and his intentions (vv. 7–9). Not one of these things is the product of his own planning and campaigning. The Father has given them to him. It is the Father who has promised him the nations as his inheritance (v. 8). It is the Father's intention that the rebellion of these nations should be crushed and that they should be brought into subjection to the king (v. 9).

The view from heaven, accordingly, yields a very striking perspective. While chaos reigns on earth as the result of humanity's arrogant rejection of God and their fumbling attempts to deal with the resulting rebellion and conflict, Jehovah and his Anointed One are seated in the heavens, confident and competent.

PAUSE FOR REFLECTION

"Therefore, you kings, be wise; be warned, you rulers of the earth." (v. 10)

Do you remember the two men looking through the prison bars? One saw mud and the other saw stars. I get worried about both classes of people represented by these two men. The muddy-eyed pessimists and the starry-eyed optimists are both off course. "Wide-eyed realism" is a better option. The realist sees earth in the light of heaven, humankind in the light of God, mud in the light of stars, and human impotence in the light of divine triumph. It is the great privilege of the believer in Christ to have the advantage of this realistic perspective.

But like all privileges, this one brings with it a great responsibility. The psalmist, who started asking questions, concludes by giving instructions. Having found some answers, he knows it is his duty to share those answers. Having the view of heaven to add to his view of earth, he knows that he must bring the "heaven view" to earth and endeavor to lift the earthbound to heaven. His ministry is to lift mud to stars and brings stars to the mud. He still stands in the mud, but he reaches to the stars.

His ministry is that of all who have a broad, realistic understanding of the situation. *"Therefore . . . be wise; be warned."* Notice carefully that the psalmist feels perfectly free to demand that those who have been in arrogant rebellion against God now take time out to gain some fresh knowledge. He insists that they exercise their minds. They must start thinking seriously about God's role in the affairs of men. But before any of us can insist that people exercise their minds, we must be equipped to give them an intelligent presentation of the message of Jehovah and his Anointed.

SERVE AND SUBMIT

*"Serve the Lord with fear and rejoice
with trembling."* (v. 11)

The message to the rebellious begins to warm up at this point. Not only does the messenger insist that they exercise their minds, but now he demands that they exert their wills and choose to serve the Lord. Note the words serve, fear, Lord, and trembling. All of these words stress the need for submission and reverence—things for which these arrogant kings were hardly noted!

That's how it is. If there is to be any change in the world situation, there must be a change of people's hearts toward the Lord. The inward change can only come when those who have understood the truth of God submit to the claims of God in their lives.

There is a strange paradox in this experience, in that submission to the Lord in fear and trembling brings rejoicing. Few people object to true joy, but most of them don't realize that true joy comes only from respectful, reverential commitment to the Lord.

EXPRESSING LOVE
"Kiss the Son . . ." (v. 12a)

The psalmist instructs these rebellious leaders to pay homage to the Son. In the Old Testament, a kiss could be both an expression of love and an acknowledgment of submission. Those who sincerely desire to serve the Lord should be willing to express to him their feelings both of love and of submission. They should be satisfied that he is Lord, they should submit to him as Lord, and they should feel very honored to be able to express their convictions openly.

Imagine the change that comes about when a former rebel, who took every opportunity to "kick" the Son, turns right around and publicly kisses the Son. Those who had followed that person's rebellious lead are now confronted with the challenge to evaluate this new dimension in their leader's life and ask what caused such a dramatic change.

The psalmist has clearly spelled out our privileges and responsibilities as believers. Aware of earth's turmoil and heaven's splendor, we should fearlessly and conscientiously alert our world to both, knowing that God has said, "Blessed are all who take refuge in him."

Psalm 8

*¹ O LORD, our Lord
how majestic is your name in all the earth!*

*You have set your glory
above the heavens.
² From the lips of children and infants
you have ordained praise
because of your enemies,
to silence the foe and the avenger.*

*³ When I consider your heavens,
the work of your fingers,
the moon and the stars,
which you have set in place,
⁴ what is man that you are mindful of him,
the son of man that you care for him?
⁵ You made him a little lower than the heavenly beings
and crowned him with glory and honor.*

*⁶ You made him ruler over the works of your hands;
you put everything under his feet:
⁷ all flocks and herds,
and the beasts of the field,
⁸ the birds of the air,
and the fish of the sea,
all that swim the paths of the seas.*

*⁹ O LORD our Lord,
how majestic is your name in all the earth!*

CHAPTER THREE

WHEN YOU DON'T LIKE BEING HUMAN

One memorable day I had lunch in England and preached twice in California. That was quite a day! I was greatly assisted by Pan American Airlines, whose flight from London to Los Angeles flew nonstop over the North Pole. The icecap is a vast area of white wilderness, unspoiled and unknown, inhabited by polar bears and seals. As far as the eye can see, it glistens in severe natural starkness.

As the plane heads south, the ice gives way to tundra. Still wilderness but not quite so formidable. After the bleak landscape of ice and snow, devoid of human habitation, it comes as a shock to see a straight and narrow road heading through the tundra to a tiny outpost.

The tundra imperceptibly gives way to prairie, the flat breadbasket of the continent. Here the signs of human intervention in the affairs of nature can be seen on every hand. The acres of cultivation are marked by different colors according to the stage of growth and harvesting of the crops.

Prairie then gives way to mountains, which give

shelter to fertile valleys full of neat, orderly vineyards and orange groves. Lean, tall, straight buildings and concrete freeways come into view as the plane descends into Los Angeles.

That journey made me proud to be human because it graphically displayed the impact of humankind on the environment. But the minute the plane door opened, a different feeling flooded me as smog invaded the cabin. My eyes, throat, lungs, and nose began to react violently to the acrid fumes.

Wiping my eyes, I confronted a customs official who would be nobody's choice for Mister Friendly. After some delay I escaped his tender mercies and climbed into a car that whisked me away to my first appointment.

Within minutes of leaving the airport, we were involved in a pileup on the Los Angeles freeway! About a dozen cars were sent careening in every direction to the accompaniment of screaming tires and people. Fists waved, epithets flew, sirens blared, and lights flashed— and I added tattered nerves and a throbbing headache to my smarting eyes and running nose.

These aspects of humanity's impact on the environment left me more ashamed than proud!

Isn't that the essence of the mystery of humanity? On the one hand, human beings are so unbelievably resourceful and skilled, and on the other hand, they can be so crude and objectionable. We humans can tame the wilds but not our temper. We drill for the oil we need from beneath frozen wastes, but then fill the air we breathe with toxic fumes from the oil we burn.

No wonder the philosophers of the ages have been asking, "What is man?" For any thinking person knows that today's world is what it is, not because of giraffes or bees, but because of us. Human beings are the enigma of our world, and without an answer to the "What is man?" question, there is little hope of answers to any of the world's problems.

WHO IS GOD?

"O LORD, our Lord how majestic is your name in all the earth!" (v. 1a–b)

David waxed philosophical one night when he had some time on his hands. He asked the question "What is man?" But he asked this question in a different context from that in which most philosophers ask it. His question came after he had been considering, not human beings, but *God* (vv. 1–3). He did not make the popular mistake of starting with people in his effort to understand human beings. He started with God and accordingly saw humanity in the correct perspective.

The one who starts with God has the opportunity to see that all things fit into a divine pattern—all things including us humans. So let us do what the psalmist did and ask the question in the correct context. In our effort to understand humanity, let's start with God.

"O LORD, our Lord" is not repetition. The first "LORD" is the name of Jehovah, as we learned in chapter 2, while the second "Lord" is God's title. Like William the Conqueror or President Lincoln, "LORD, Lord" speaks of God's name and title, and both are majestic. LORD, Jehovah, means "the self-existent one." It is in this very name that lies a great clue to the meaning of humanity. For despite what humanistic thinkers would have us believe, we humans are not self-sufficient. We cannot claim to have all the answers, and we definitely are not the final authority. The Lord alone is all these things, and, therefore, any theory of existence that starts anywhere else than with the Lord must be erroneous.

God's title of Lord means "master." "How majestic is your name in all the earth!" So once again, we, as creatures of earth, are thrust into the position of acknowledging one Master who is over all rather than innumerable human masters who feel they are invincible and infallible.

Humanistic reasoning resists these divine principles, of course, but I can't understand why. Personally, if I were a humanist and could see what a mess humans have made, I would be thrilled to hear of an alternative. But strangely, this is not the case. Many of the Lord's opponents march on, bravely and hopelessly endeavoring to salvage humanity from the ruinous products of our own ingenuity.

IT'S NOT ALL UP TO US

"You have set your glory above the heavens." (v. 1c–d)

Another problem is that we humans tend to be desperately earthbound in our thinking. We believe we must carry all the problems of the world on our own shoulders because there aren't any other shoulders on which to place them. We feel that all the answers have to come from our finite wisdom because there aren't any other places from which they could be expected. Most of us have little concept of the miraculous, no idea of the supernatural other than vague superstition and arm's-length interest in such things as ESP, and no expectation whatsoever of the superhuman intervention of God in human affairs.

How wrong can we be! God has set his "glory above the heavens." Jehovah our Lord has glory that fills the heavens far beyond what mortal eye can see. He has untold riches of being that boggle the mind and surpass description. How puny, therefore, is the human philosophy that ties itself to human resources and denies itself the possibility of glory from above the heavens!

PRAISE FROM INFANTS

"From the lips of children and infants you have ordained praise . . ." (v. 2a–b)

Our great God is very direct in his dealings with us. If we will not praise him, then it will come from children.

There is something deliciously uncomplicated about the uninhibited way children let you know what they think and how they feel. Infants can't say much, but they communicate very effectively. They may be suffering from not enough moisture at one end, too much at the other, or wind in-between. If you pour it in, mop it up, or burp it out, peace will reign.

God, working through the *"lips of children and infants,"* is letting us know that things are basically simple and should be dealt with accordingly. Sad to say, but as the years go by, children tend to learn how to be more sophisticated and complicated. They learn how to produce neuroses, psychoses, and thromboses. In fact, the more one sees how adept people are at fouling up their lives, the more one wishes they could stay as fresh and as uncomplicated as they once were.

If only we could stop getting so smart, so sophisticated, and so enthralled with our own undeniable abilities, we might be able to save ourselves a lot of trouble in life. If only we could hear the truth of God in simple terms instead of relying on human error pronounced with erudition, things would be so much better. Many a prominent executive hears more sense spoken by his own five-year-old son or daughter in prayer at bedtime than he hears all day from the people he is paying to advise him. Not that the five-year-old understands the intricacies of high finance, but he or she certainly knows enough to grasp the necessity of simple faith.

God speaks to sophisticated people, ordaining praise through the mouths of infants. But sophisticated people are usually preoccupied with more important things and tend to dismiss these humble events with a kiss and a "That's cute, honey."

SILENCING OUR ENEMIES

". . . because of your enemies, to silence the foe and the avenger." (v. 2c–d)

God has his enemies, and they are our enemies as well. Unfortunately, some of us have been fooled into thinking that our worst enemies are not real, and as a result, we are basically defenseless against them.

Simon Peter discovered to his dismay that his well-intentioned attempt to dissuade Jesus from heading into danger was actually a tool of Satan to thwart the purposes of God. Satan can use nice people to do bad things. He is slick, sly, crafty, and cunning.

If we don't recognize the reality of God's enemies, there is no way that we will accept God's unlikely methods of defeating them. God has his way of dealing with his enemies, and it is not our way. The Lord uses "the foolish things of the world to shame the wise" (1 Corinthians 1:27) and brings power from infants to *"silence the foe and the avenger."* Once again we see that, from the divine perspective, we have things all wrong.

CONSIDER THE HEAVENS

"When I consider your heavens, the work of your fingers, the moon and the stars, which you have set in place, what is man that you are mindful of him, the son of man that you care for him?" (vv. 3–4)

All through history, people have gazed at the heavens. Sometimes we have gotten into trouble, as Galileo did. Other times we have derived great insights, as the Magi did. In recent times, we have set our sights on the heavens in a new way. With consummate skill and courage, we have begun exploring the heavens. We have accepted the challenge of space. Politically, scientifically, economically, and occasionally spiritually, we have explored the heavens that have enthralled us since the beginning of time.

The first American astronaut came back from space believing in God more than when he took off. The first Russian cosmonaut came back more convinced in the *non*existence of God than when he left. The reverent soul of the astronaut saw order and beauty and attributed both to an orderly, beautiful God. The cosmonaut didn't expect to find God up there and was neither surprised nor disappointed that he didn't see him. Both men, of course, were acting on presuppositions. But one of these presuppositions was wrong. If the believer in God is wrong, he has lost nothing; but if the unbeliever is wrong, he has lost everything!

When the psalmist looked at the heavens, he didn't do so to bolster his presuppositions; he was moved to profound questions. He gazed upon the galaxies with an inquiring mind, and his reverent soul humbly asked, *"When I consider your heavens . . . what is man that you are mindful of him?"* Or, as the New Living Translation renders it, "What are mortals that you should think of us?"

I like this approach to the "What is man?" question. It has content and humility and approaches the problem of existence with a deep sense of wonder and reverence. The question is asked in the context of the universe as a whole and in the context of the Creator as the one who has the answer. When this great philosophical question is asked this way, it can be answered.

GOD MADE US!
"You made him . . ." (v. 5a)

For years many of our best brains have contended that humankind is the chance product of circumstances in a universe that is itself the freak result of unknown occurrences. This humanistic view has been particularly popular among those who find it hard or uncomfortable to believe in God. They have been able to free themselves from religious concepts and systems of morality and to produce their own substitutes. Their lifestyles have reflected these substitute standards and in most instances have proved extremely attractive to contemporary society.

There is one problem, however, that unbelieving people have been unable to avoid. While many find it refreshing and liberating to be free of God, to believe that they have made God in *their* own image and that therefore they can dismiss him with impunity, it is at the same time *dehumanizing* to believe that humans are not a logical entity with a rational base. It is humiliating to be convinced that humans are an accident and are therefore of little importance. The theories that lead people to believe that they "just happened" must also logically lead them to believe that they are meaningless. And that is dehumanizing.

But there is nothing dehumanizing about the psalmist's understanding of humankind. The fact that God made us is his great conviction.

Despite all the harsh attacks on the biblical view of humanity, it must be stated quite firmly that nowhere else is such a high view of humanity taught. The Bible insists that we are the intelligent product of an intelligent Creator. The Bible never gives the impression that we are simply a puzzle living in the middle of a muddle.

JUST BELOW THE ANGELS

". . . a little lower than the heavenly beings . . ." (v. 5a)

Not only does this psalm reveal that we are made by God, it also reveals our position in the order of creation. *"A little lower than the heavenly beings"* is a whole lot better than "slightly better than the apes!" Let's get the order straight: God, angelic beings, human beings, animals, and vegetables.

The major sphere of operation for both God and the angels is in the heavens. There is much that we don't understand about spiritual forces, both benevolent and malevolent, but we know that they exist. Scripture is clear on that in both the Old and the New Testament. There is much we cannot grasp about the "heavenlies," but we know that such spheres of being and activity are real. We do, however, know about human beings and the earth, and we learn from this psalm that our role on earth is very similar to, and only slightly inferior to, the role of the angels in heaven. Hebrews 1:14 tells us that angels are "ministering spirits" who serve in dimensions that are beyond human limitations. We are also ministering spirits in the dimensions within which *we* are equipped to serve. God made us a little lower than the angels for this very purpose. We function on earth as angels function in heaven.

CROWNED WITH GLORY

". . . and crowned him with glory and honor." (v. 5b)

If we feel peeved that we were made a little lower than some other created beings, we can cheer up because God's Word tells us that in our own sphere, earth, we have no equal. Within the context of the earth, we are the pinnacle of divine creation, the beings made to exhibit great glory and receive great honor. The unique glory of humanity is that we were made "in the image of God," specially equipped in body, soul, and spirit to know God and be known by him.

God has always had a special place in his heart for human beings, whom he made superior to any other part of his earthly creation. God has shown down through the ages that he delights in us as he delights in no other part of his workmanship. God has chosen to have the kind of fellowship with human beings that he has with nothing and no one else.

Another psalm tells us that we are "fearfully and wonderfully made" (Psalm 139:14). We had to be made that way in order to be equipped for divine fellowship. It takes a *mind* that can understand something of the immensity of God, a *heart* that will respond to what the mind has grasped, and a *will* that can acknowledge in action what the mind has grasped and the heart has felt. Intellectually honored, emotionally glorious, and volitionally unique, we humans are truly *"crowned with glory and honor."*

GOD MADE US TO BE RULERS

"You made him ruler over the works of your hands; you put everything under his feet: all flocks and herds, and the beasts of the field, the birds of the air, and the fish of the sea, all that swim the paths of the seas." (vv. 6–8)

If we humans have been made supreme in the earthly realm and have been gifted uniquely for a special relationship with our Creator, it is no surprise to discover that God has given us a superb role in his plan. Our role is to rule over the works of God's hands. The psalmist limits his list of the works of God's hands to various types of animal life, but we must not assume that our mandate is limited to these areas. He goes on to say that

God has put all things *"under [our] feet."*

We don't know exactly what happened in the beginning at Creation. We will never know this side of heaven
exactly what God did, how he did it, how long he took, or
what methods he used. It is unlikely that we will ever har-
monize adequately our discoveries in the scientific realm
with the statements of theologians. Nevertheless, one
thing is quite clear: God made a fantastic world and set us
humans loose in it to develop and explore it to our fullest
potential. Our unbelievable mandate was to use our God-
given talent to discover the abundant resources of earth
and to adapt all that we found to the development of
God's creation in every sphere. What a challenge to our
creativity and ingenuity!

And what a remarkable job we have done! At some
point in antiquity, we took four round stones, stuck two
stakes through them, added a connecting seat, and the original Cadillac was born. We began to build roads and
bridges and dams, houses and cities, ships and cars. We
explored the wildernesses and found coal and oil and iron
and salt. We made contact lenses and laser beams and tele-
visions and computers. We found cures for tuberculosis
and vaccines for polio. We opened hearts and transplanted
kidneys, made music and painted pictures. We have come a
long way from the day when God made us to have domin-
ion. In fact, we have subdued everything in the world and
then headed for space, looking for other worlds to conquer.

There is only one thing we haven't subdued: we have

never learned to subdue ourselves. And therein lies the root of the human dilemma.

But Where Did We Go Wrong?

Human beings are the arch-producers but also the arch-polluters. We manufacture scalpels and submarines. We heal and harm, educate and exterminate. We can overflow with humanitarian goodwill and then explode in inhumanity toward other humans. At the office we can be the essence of civility to a client, then we go home and become the ultimate in rudeness to our spouse.

Without us, this world would be infinitely better and infinitely worse. Infinitely better because without us there would be no war and no divorce and no heartache. If there were no human beings, there would be no pollution and no crime. There would be only clear streams, wide open horizons, virgin forests, and natural development.

But without us, the world would be infinitely worse because there would be no art or music or literature. There never would have been the joy of a newborn baby's cry, the thrill of a wedding, the glow of love. Minerals would lie hidden forever in the earth, oil untapped, and coral reefs unknown. Diamonds would never have been cut to reflect a thousand sparkles. There would be no language or printing or books or verse. There would have been no cathedrals with soaring arches and no one to capture majestic sunsets on film. It would be an odd world without us.

We are both the masters of the earth's resources and the masterminds behind many of the world's ills. Any discussion of the great question "What is man?" must take all of this into account. There is enough good and brilliance in the human race to convince an honest person that we were made in the image of God. However, there are many things about us humans to suggest that God would resent being held responsible for us! The image of God is discernible, but it is a broken image, a distorted reflection of what he originally intended for the pinnacle of his creation.

It Happened at the Fall

To my mind there is no adequate explanation for the puzzle of the human race other than the biblical explanation that, though made in the perfection of God for the glory of God, we rejected that high calling and fell into something sadly inferior. Any theory of chance development must fall on hard times when it is confronted with the obvious facts of the human race's uniqueness and unquestioned superiority over anything else in the created world.

Even with the most accommodating attitude, it is hard to see how anyone can really put the inventor of a computer in the same class as a dolphin. Chimpanzees can certainly peel bananas with dexterity, but does that really put them in the same class with brain surgeons? Chimps and dolphins aren't in our class when it comes to ingenuity and skill, but they don't have our evil propensities either.

There is something about humans that isn't found in animals. It's called evil genius. It takes a Fall into sin to produce a human race that retains some vestiges of God-given grandeur and at the same time demonstrates callous indifference, gross abuse, frightening fierceness, and cold, calculating hate.

What Can Be Done?

We find the answer to the human dilemma in a New Testament passage that quotes from this very psalm: "But we see Jesus, who was made a little lower than the angels, now crowned with glory and honor because he suffered death" (Hebrews 2:9). The Lord from glory, our Lord Jesus, was for a little while made lower than the angels; that is, he took human form, for the express purpose of tasting death for us. Why was this necessary? It was necessary in order that "by his death he might destroy him who holds the power of death—that is, the devil—and free those who all their lives were held in slavery by their fear of death" (Hebrews 2:14–15). There's the clue. Humankind, the great and glorious ruler of the world, is in bondage to "him who holds the power of death—that is, the devil."

Human beings, made in the image of God to rule and reign as the divine agent in charge of earth, rejected their privileged place and exposed themselves to the devil. The devil took brilliant people and began to manipulate them and the world they inhabited—to the glory of the devil and the ultimate destruction of both humankind and the world. But Jesus came and through his death and resurrection dealt the devil a body blow. He offered freedom from the devil's domination to all who will acknowledge him and reject the devil.

Deliverance from the devil means considerably more then eventual bliss in heaven. It is much more than the proverbial "pie in the sky when you die." It has to do with being free from the devil's influence to such a degree that we can become more like the people we were initially created to be; free to subdue the earth for the purposes of God rather than for human greed; liberated from devilish dynamics and brought under the power of divine principle.

BRINGING US INTO GLORY

So where is it all going to end? Though we have squandered our great potential as humans and have served the devil instead of serving God, God through Christ can release us from evil and bring us once again under his benevolent control. As he does so, he begins leading us nearer and nearer to the glory he intended for us in the first place. He brings "his many children into glory" (Hebrews 2:10 NLT).

Meanwhile, as our Lord is leading us to glory, we need to be giving our time and effort to teaching our fellow human beings what they, too, can be in Christ.

Psalm 11

¹ *In the* LORD *I take refuge.*
How then can you say to me:
"Flee like a bird to your mountain.
² *For look, the wicked bend their bows;*
they set their arrows against the strings
to shoot from the shadows
at the upright in heart.
³ *When the foundations are being destroyed,*
what can the righteous do?"

⁴ *The* LORD *is in his holy temple;*
the LORD *is on his heavenly throne.*
He observes the sons of men;
his eyes examine them.
⁵ *The* LORD *examines the righteous,*
but the wicked and those who love violence
his soul hates.
⁶ *On the wicked he will rain*
fiery coals and burning sulfur;
a scorching wind will be their lot.
⁷ *For the* LORD *is righteous,*
he loves justice;
upright men will see his face.

CHAPTER FOUR

WHEN ALL YOU KNOW
IS DISCOURAGEMENT

Bumper stickers sometimes convey messages that are totally contradicted by the people driving the cars. One night when I was driving in the pouring rain, I was almost run off the road by a car that passed me where there was no room to pass. Through my rain-covered windshield, I was just able to decipher the bumper sticker: "See you in church on Sunday."

Another day I was exhorted to "Honk if you love Jesus" by the bumper sticker on the car ahead of me at the traffic light. So I did, and the driver turned around and shook his fist at me!

A recent cartoon in a national magazine showed a little man in a car whose sticker read, "Honk if you believe in anything." He represents a lot of people in our world who are downright despondent and discouraged, people who have nothing solid to believe in.

No doubt there is much to discourage people in today's troubled world. But there is no reason why anyone should stay discouraged. There are many good answers to discouragement, and some of them can be

found in Psalm 11. David had plenty of practice coping with discouraging situations and gave us the wise benefit of his experience.

THE URGE TO FLEE

"In the LORD I take refuge. How then can you say to me:
'Flee like a bird to your mountain.'" (v. 1)

During his life, David often found himself in such tight corners that discretion rather than valor would appear to have been the wisest course. In the difficult situation underlying this psalm, David was not helped by a group of anonymous advisers who suggested that, as things were so hopeless, he should pack his bags and run for his life. In all probability he had been tempted to think that way himself.

Some time ago some kids from the congregation brought a youngster into my office just as I was about to go into the Sunday evening service. They said he was taking off for Texas and wondered if I could make an announcement in the church to see if anyone was going in his direction and would give him a ride. I pointed out to them that the possibilities of someone leaving Wisconsin for Texas on a Sunday night were remote, but I would be happy to help him in some other way if possible. As I talked with him for a few minutes, his story came tumbling out: parents divorced, mother remarried, stepfather belligerent, conflict at home, his schoolwork suffering—then dropping out of school, getting a job, becoming unemployed, and finally running away. And he was only sixteen.

People have a natural tendency to *"flee like a bird to [the] mountain"* when things get tough, when the going is really intolerable. And it isn't only young people who feel this way. My phone often rings late at night. Usually the call is from a potential suicide or an alcoholic. Either way, the person concerned is fleeing to his or her mountain. Reality has become too much, and a flight from reality is seemingly the only alternative for those who feel so overwhelmed.

The Calm Voice of Faith

Be careful that you do not miss the main point of this psalm. The whole psalm is a response to the pessimistic advice he has been receiving concerning his discouraging circumstances. There is a note of outrage in his response: "I take refuge in the Lord, so how can you tell me to flee?"

David's words could, of course, have been words of blustering self-confidence or frightened belligerence, but in this case they are not. David speaks here with the calm voice of faith: *"In the LORD I take refuge."*

In the New Testament the words *faith* and *believe* are very common, but in the Old Testament *trust* is the more common word. In fact, it occurs more than 150 times. Today, we have developed some ideas about faith that are somewhat disturbing. To have faith or to believe is little more than agreeing with certain facts. To believe or have faith in the Lord is, for these people, nothing more than giving mental assent to the facts of God's existence. But the Old Testament word *trust* reminds us that there is much more to faith than intellectual assent. Real faith trusts what it believes. It stakes its very life on the object of its faith.

My dad believed implicitly that airplanes could fly. He had no alternative because he had seen them doing so on many occasions. But he was adamant that he would "never set foot in one of those contraptions." And he never did. He went to glory without the help of an airplane. He believed, but his belief never extended to trust.

David's answer to discouragement is not believing something *about* the Lord, but putting trust *in* the Lord. Let's look at what the act of trusting involves.

Three different Hebrew words are translated *trust* throughout the psalms. In this psalm, the Hebrew word used for trust meant "to take refuge in." As soon as believers start talking about taking refuge in the Lord, their opponents jump for joy. "There you are," they say. "You have wishbones instead of backbones. You're so terribly inadequate that you have to manufacture a God to help you cope with life."

People who talk like that need to understand one thing. They must be made to see that *everyone is inadequate* at some point in his or her experience. No one is exempt from the fact that sooner or later in life, they will face something they can't handle. This they cannot deny. Eventually, even the most self-possessed person will crumble. Tragedy, old age, sickness—there comes some point in all of our lives when we realize we've gone as far as we can. The realistic thing to do, therefore, is to admit this now and start planning for it. As soon as we do this, we'll find many other areas of inadequacy of which we may not have been aware.

We all have basic needs of such things as security—some people more than others. We show our need for security in different ways. Some people need a secure home situation, a retreat where they can be in their own place and do their own thing. Others need to be told how much they are appreciated, how well they are doing, and how invaluable they are. Without this, they tend to fall apart. Little children drag dirty security blankets with them. Many business executives appear to need opulent offices or status symbol automobiles to make them feel secure.

In addition to security needs of this nature, we have real spiritual needs. When it comes to coping with sickness of soul, limousines and expensive houses are of no more use than security blankets. There has to be a place of refuge to which the overextended person can go. There has to be a Lord in whom refuge can be found.

People tell me that I give the impression of coping quite well with pressures and problems. Some say that they won't come to me for advice because either I don't have problems or apparently I cope with them so effectively that they feel ashamed coming to me. The fact of the matter is that life has taught me to take refuge in the Lord.

Unashamedly I run to him. In fact, if it were not for the ready access I have to him, I would never survive in the ministry. The pressures would be more than I could take. Whenever I begin to feel pressed in from every side, I hide myself away with him. I crawl into a corner and talk to him. When the heat is on, I pull the drapes and commune with him. I take refuge in him. And he never lets me down.

Leaning on the Lord

Another word translated *trust* means "to lean upon." We read in Psalm 9:10 that "Those who know your name will trust in you." Shortly after arriving in Milwaukee, I met with a group of young people. After I had discussed the things of God with them for some time, a young woman who was sitting on the floor burst out, "I can't stand another minute of this." I thought she was referring to her uncomfortable position on the floor. But she went on, "All this talk about God is nonsense. God is the result of weak people looking for a crutch. Your God is nothing more than a crutch."

She was really angry, so I chose not to interrupt. Eventually, when she appeared to be about through with her monologue, I said, "You are one of the most interesting persons I have ever met. If you were skiing and broke your leg, you would be taken to the hospital and have your leg set in a cast. The doctor would then give you a stick of wood with a rubber cup on one end, an armpit-shaped pad on the other, and a handle in the middle. Presumably you would object violently at being given a crutch! Crutches are not to be despised; they are to be appreciated, because they meet needs perfectly. Anyone who admits to a need welcomes the answer to that need. You are no more against God than you are against crutches. You simply won't admit that you need support."

This is a problem for many people. Even when it is obvious that they are craving support, they deny it. They try to cover up their feelings in many ways, but they must learn to admit to their needs and learn that the Lord is the one on whom they can lean. This is the life of faith, the experience of trust.

I recall one particular man who was deeply discouraged. He tried to hide his very real problems. He tried to run away from his crushing load. Whenever I saw him, I shared the things of the Lord with him, encouraging him to lean on the Lord and to find in him the support he needed. But he always held back. It wasn't that he didn't "believe." He was a firm believer in God's existence, but he felt that he had to try to find all the solutions himself and battle the insuperable odds all alone. I feared for him as I would fear for anyone who was not in a position to say, "*In the LORD I take refuge.*"

Rolling on the Lord

In Psalm 22 we find a remarkable prophetic statement concerning the crucifixion of our Lord. Later, while on the cross in dying agony, Jesus made reference to this psalm, and, strangely, even his detractors quoted it too: "He trusts in the LORD; let the LORD rescue him" (Psalm 22:8; see Matthew 27:43). Here this word *trust* means literally "to roll upon."

The enemies of the Lord Jesus knew many things about him, and one of the things they knew was that Jesus "rolled himself upon Jehovah." They didn't like the fact that he trusted his Father in heaven for everything. In fact, they ridiculed him even on the cross. While their vindictiveness comes through with startling clarity in this passage of Scripture, the fact of the Lord's relationship with the Father is even more startling. There were situations in Christ's life through which he moved with absolute confidence as no one has ever moved. The reserves of strength he exhibited and the fortitude he displayed have amazed men and women down through the centuries. But never forget how he did it. He trusted in God.

An obvious question comes to mind: if Jesus needed to operate this way, what makes me think I can get by without rolling my burdens on the Lord?

One of the first stories I remember hearing from a pulpit described an old woman going to market carrying a large basket of dairy produce. A local farmer riding along to market in his wagon stopped and offered her a ride, which she gladly accepted. After a few minutes, the farmer noticed the woman was sitting there hugging her large, heavy basket. When he suggested that she put it on the floor, she replied, "Oh no, thank you, I'd prefer to hold it on my knee and keep the weight off the horse."

Go on, laugh! But don't laugh too loudly because, if you are like me, you probably do the same thing with the Lord. You refuse to roll your burdens on the Lord. But you must do just that, if you are ever going to cope with the discouragements and the disappointments that life will bring you way.

David had an alternative approach to discouragement. His reaction to despondent advice was quick and powerful. "In the LORD I take refuge. How then can you say to me: 'Flee like a bird to your mountain?'" David's trust was in God.

Who Is Trusting What?

We must not get the impression that only believers trust when things get tough. Everybody trusts something. "Some trust in chariots and some in horses, but we trust in the name of the LORD our God" (Psalm 20:7). Everybody trusts something, but the things they trust in vary considerably. Tanks and missiles or material acquisitions replace horses and chariots as objects of trust today. Many of our contemporaries are despondent about the world situation. Before its collapse, the Soviet Union was locked with the United States in a massive arms race to try to produce some international stability. Many people trust in "luck."

Others just seem to have an inbred trust that somebody will think of something.

It should be obvious from history that not everything in which people trust is worthy of that trust. Thousands trusted Hitler and were destroyed. Millions have voted for various political leaders and have been deeply disillusioned. Some have trusted in faith healers but have died anyway. The foolish trust in luck, only to find that Lady Luck is cruel.

People may have a great willingness to lean on luck or take refuge in tanks, but that is no guarantee that all will be well. The very trust that they place in these things may lead to disaster, not because trust is disastrous, but because they are trusting in untrustworthy things.

This leads us to consider the most important thing about trust: its object. My dad used to tell the story of a big, somewhat overweight Sunday-school teacher who placed a chair on the platform in full view of about five hundred children and said, "Boys and girls, I am now going to demonstrate what trust is." With that he threw his great weight on the unoffending chair, which promptly collapsed below him. To the unspeakable delight of the children, he landed flat on his back amid the ruins, with his feet in the air. One scruffy kid with tears running down his face exclaimed, "This is better than the movies!"

The large demonstrator of trust regained his feet and his composure, held his hands up to silence the crowd, and said, "I tried to demonstrate one thing to you and managed to demonstrate two. I showed you what trust is, but I also showed you that you must be careful what you put your trust in."

Exactly. Whenever you feel discouraged, put your trust in the Lord.

WHEN THINGS GET TOUGH

"Look, the wicked bend their bows; they set their arrows against the strings. . . ." (v. 2a–b)

David's "encouragers" noted that there were some people out to get him. Surely this had not escaped David's attention. The psalmist points out that his enemies were wicked at heart and ready to attack. Do you sometimes feel like David? When the arrows start falling around you thick and fast, it might seem you are being used for target practice. And perhaps your first reaction is to run for cover. But running for cover is not quite the same as running from the field altogether.

Sometimes circumstances pile in on people to such an extent that it seems there's no end to what might happen. A young wife and mother in our congregation was rushed to the hospital because a lump had suddenly appeared in her throat. Malignancy was on everyone's mind. Emergency surgery followed. The tumor was removed, and lab tests showed it was benign. The family felt great relief, until their six week-old baby started to run temperatures of 105 degrees. Meningitis was the diagnosis, and once again the young parents were under tremendous pressure. All this came after severe problems in other areas relating to work and family.

Things can get tough, and the tougher things get, the harder it is to resist discouragement.

WHO IS DESTROYING OUR FOUNDATIONS?

"When the foundations are being destroyed, what can the righteous do?" (v. 3)

It is difficult to say which foundations David's advisers meant in verse 3. Whenever foundations of any kind are destroyed, the result can be a horrible sinking feeling.

Many believe that the foundations of society are being destroyed today—foundations such as:

- integrity
- honesty
- moral and ethical standards
- the sanctity and permanence of marriage
- the value of a stable family and home

As these foundations start to crumble, what do many of these people do? They flee like a bird to their mountain. They quit. They decide that they will concentrate on protecting themselves amid the inevitable disintegration. They write off society and yield to their fear and discouragement.

"What can the righteous do?" I get the impression that David's friends asked this question with a note of pathetic

defeat. Far be it from me to criticize these unknown friends, but I believe the righteous should never quit, no matter how daunting the odds. Though we may face our "modern-day" Goliaths, the same God who stood by David stands by our side to give us victory. I have a firm conviction that, while the believer will inevitably be as open to arrows of defeat and prone to discouragement as the next person, the similarity should end there. When the discouraged flee for the mountains, Christians should take another course and talk like David: "In the LORD I take refuge" (v. 1).

THE LORD WHO INTERCEDES
"The LORD is in his holy temple . . ." (v. 4a)

David describes the Lord as being *"in his holy temple."* This immediately brings to my mind a picture of the priest quietly and efficiently going about his business in the temple, offering sacrifices and prayers on behalf of the people. The Lord Jesus Christ is shown in many roles in Scripture, and his ministry as our Great High Priest is one of the most beautiful. Our ascended Lord "always lives to intercede" for us (Hebrews 7:25). One aspect of Christ's present ministry in heaven is praying on our behalf.

This has a direct bearing on what we should do when we become despondent. Should we flee to our mountain, or should we trust the Lord who is praying for us? The answer is quite plain. To flee is unthinkable in such circumstances. To lean upon the fact of our Lord's intercession, to "roll upon" this High Priest, to take refuge in this temple is the way to go.

THE LORD WHO REIGNS

". . . the LORD is on his heavenly throne." (v. 4b)

Nebuchadnezzar was a dreamer who forgot what he had dreamed. But he didn't say, "It was only a dream." He sent for his professional dream interpreters and told them they would be cut in little pieces if they didn't come up with both the dream and its interpretation quickly.

Daniel then came on the scene and, like the rest of the men in his field of prophecy, he was facing an "early retirement." However, instead of being despondent at the situation he said, "There is a God in heaven" (Daniel 2:28) and proceeded to tackle the problem that had all the other wise men of Babylon fearing for their lives.

The story of Daniel is a great one for people who have demanding employers! It's also great for all who need to be reminded that God does reign in human affairs. There is a throne in heaven, and there is an all-powerful God on that throne. Trust in the Ruling One lifts the despondent and stops them from having to flee to their mountains.

THE LORD WHO EXAMINES

"He observes the sons of men; his eyes examine them."
(v. 4c–d)

Not only does God watch us, *"his eyes examine"* us carefully. Now there's a strange and beautiful expression. I didn't understand it until I was talking to a group of students one day about spiritual realities. They were listening intently and skeptically. Intent on my every word, they had narrowed their eyes to tiny slits. Their eyelids were examining me, carefully weighing me, evaluating, checking. Critically!

Have you ever observed a trainer watching a young boxer? He stands in the corner studying every move, every blow, waiting to see how much his youngster can take, ready to jump to his assistance at any given moment.

There are those whom the Lord views critically, as the students viewed me. His eyes examine them. There are others who know that God's eyes examine them not critically but lovingly. Both the righteous and the unrighteous know God's searching gaze. To the one it speaks judgment, but to the others, who know God well, his gaze conveys loving concern.

The composite picture of the Lord that we now have is enough to encourage even the most despondent person to pause and reflect. But there is one final aspect of the knowledge of God that we should mention.

THE HOPE OF SEEING HIS FACE

"For the LORD is righteous, he loves justice; upright men will see his face." (v. 7)

Depending on which translation of the Bible you use, you may read the last verse of the psalm as "his countenance beholds the upright" (NKJV) or "upright men will see his face" (NIV). Both are true of course and do justice to the text.

Let's examine the second possibility. Hope is the ingredient that is missing in many a despondent person's life. But it is not missing in the trusting believer's experience because in addition to knowing God as High Priest and King and Judge, the believer knows that one day he or she will behold the face of their Lord. This is the glorious hope of the trusting soul.

So if you feel like quitting your job, leaving your wife, hitting the road, dropping out of school, transferring your church membership, emigrating to another country, or moving into your bomb shelter, *don't*! At least, not in discouragement! Hold on a minute and ask yourself, "Have I allowed all these things to get on top of me so much that I have forgotten to trust the Lord?" When you have asked yourself that question, really try to answer it. Then decide whether you should flee to your mountain, or whether you should look your discouragements straight in the eye and shout, "In the Lord I take refuge!"

Psalm 19

1 *The heavens declare the glory of God;*
the skies proclaim the work of his hands.
2 *Day after day they pour forth speech;*
night after night they display knowledge.
3 *There is no speech or language*
where their voice is not heard.
4 *Their voice goes out into all the earth,*
their words to the ends of the world.

In the heavens he has pitched a tent for the sun,
5 *which is like a bridegroom coming forth from his pavilion,*
like a champion rejoicing to run his course.
6 *It rises at one end of the heavens*
and makes its circuit to the other;
nothing is hidden from its heat.

7 *The law of the LORD is perfect,*
reviving the soul.
The statutes of the LORD are trustworthy,
making wise the simple.
8 *The precepts of the LORD are right,*
giving joy to the heart.
The commands of the LORD are radiant,
giving light to the eyes.
9 *The fear of the LORD is pure,*
enduring forever.
The ordinances of the LORD are sure
and altogether righteous.
10 *They are more precious than gold,*
than much pure gold;
they are sweeter than honey,
than honey from the comb.
11 *By them is your servant warned;*
in keeping them there is great reward.

12 Who can discern his errors?
Forgive my hidden faults.
13 Keep your servant also from willful sins;
may they not rule over me.
Then will I be blameless,
innocent of great transgression.

14 May the words of my mouth and the meditation of my heart
be pleasing in your sight,
O LORD, my Rock and my Redeemer.

CHAPTER FIVE

WHEN YOU WONDER
WHERE TO GET ANSWERS

Sometimes I sit down and think about the fact that our world is rather ridiculous. Depending on how I feel at the time, my reaction varies from laughing to crying. Have you ever thought how silly it is that millions of us should be on a little planet spinning in space? We don't know where it's heading, we don't get along with one another, most of us have never seen much of the rest of the planet, and the majority of us don't really care about it. Just so long as we have food in our stomachs, a roof over our heads, and money in our pockets, the spinning world can go its crazy way for all we care. We can't stop its spinning; we can't change its course. There's not a thing we can do about its relation to anything. We're stuck with it and on it, except for a handful of people who have taken desperately expensive trips to get away from it for a week or two.

GOD HAS SPOKEN THROUGH THE HEAVENS

"The heavens declare the glory of God; the skies proclaim the work of his hands. Day after day they pour forth speech; night after night they display knowledge. There is no

speech or language where their voice is not heard. Their voice goes out into all the earth, their words to the ends of the world." (vv. 1–4)

However, some people will not settle for the indifferent approach. They are unwilling to spin aimlessly in space, caring nothing about why they spin. From time long past there has been a strange breed of people who love to take long walks or sit under trees, scratching their heads and thinking. "Philosophers," we call them. They are inquisitive people who try to work out principles that lie behind human conduct and thought. They endeavor to seek out meaning and knowledge and unravel the mysteries of existence and the universe.

Fascinating people they are. Next time you see someone walking in deep thought, get into conversation with him or her. You may learn something. On the other hand, you may find that those people have not come up with any answers. The more they think, the more uncertain they may become about the mysteries of the universe in which we live. This is not uncommon among thinkers, as is indicated by the fact that thinkers spend much of their time thinking about what other thinkers think and deciding that they think others are thinking wrong! Philosophy can be confusing and discouraging.

The problem is knowing where to start. If a clever thinker says to herself as she looks at her reflection in a pool, "There I am; at least, I think I am there," she starts with a rather shaky premise. If she goes on from there to try to understand everything around her in terms of her own being, she will end up with a closed and limited system of thought that may well be brilliant but will certainly be inadequate.

Revelation Versus Speculation

There is another approach to the whole business of thought about existence and meaning. Instead of starting with the human mind trying to reach into mysteries it cannot comprehend, one may listen to God. This approach is exactly the opposite of speculation. It is called *revelation*. Instead of being nothing more than the product of human ingenuity, revelation is the product of divine thought—eternal, infinite, limitless.

It's like a young schoolboy finding a calculator in a field, sitting down under a tree, scratching his head, and speculating about what he found. *It's the controls for a flying saucer*, he muses, *and if I press this button, a giant spacecraft will appear.* Good speculation, but inaccurate.

Having tried that without success, he thinks again. *I know! It's a dictionary that fell out of a flying saucer, and if I press enough of these buttons I might learn to speak Martian.* Good speculation again, but learning Martian soon proves to be as difficult and boring as learning Latin. And the calculator is no good for either!

More speculation is necessary. Unless, of course, a little man with a shabby raincoat and big glasses comes by, sees the boy with the calculator, and says, "Thank goodness, you've found the calculator I lost. I've been using that thing for years. Here, let me show you what it is and how it works." That will mean the end of speculation and the beginning of revelation for the boy.

The big fly in the ointment of this approach is the question of whether God actually has spoken or will speak. And if so, will we understand his language? The clear statement of Scripture is that God has spoken, that he continues to speak, and that we can understand him. If this is true, it must be one of the most exciting things known to humankind. If the great Creator has left some indication of what he had in mind for us originally, and what he is continuing to do for us, that information must surely be the most important information available to humankind.

God speaks through creation. *"There is no speech or language"* in all the earth where the silent testimony of creation *"is not heard."* Creation speaks of God with unrelenting force and clarity. Everyone on the face of this earth has been confronted in one way or another with the silent voice of God's majestic creation.

The Heavens Speak Out

Red sky at night, shepherd's delight.
Red sky at morning, shepherd's warning.

Variations of this couplet are known around the world. In this sense at least, many people accept the statement that the heavens declare things to us. Meteorologists look to the heavens to declare what a day will bring forth, and this information is broadcast to millions through the media. But the psalmist has much more in mind than weather forecasts. He speaks of the heavens declaring "the glory of God."

To the reverent observer, the heavens speak of numerous aspects of God's glory. But I believe the heavens speak to the less reverent as well. For instance, any informed observer of the heavens, reverent or not, knows that at any one time only about 2,500 stars are visible to the naked eye, yet this number increases infinitely, depending on the quality of telescope available. In fact, the more we study the heavens, the more immense they appear. There is no discernible end to them.

We tend to forget scientific terms like light-years once we graduate from high school. Let me remind you that for some reason known only to God, light travels at the remarkable speed of 186,282 miles per second. Multiply that by 60 (seconds in a minute), then by 60 (minutes in an hour), then by 24 (hours in a day), then by 365 (days in a year), and you have the distance light travels in a year: approximately 6 trillion miles. Sirius, one of our bright friends, is about 54 trillion miles, or 9 light-years, away from us! If we will allow the immensity of the heavens to speak to us, we will begin to think of the immensity of the Creator.

I happen to be convinced that one of the best things that we can learn from any source is that there is a great and glorious God who has given us some little idea of his glory by letting us see something of his creative genius. I also believe that the revelation of his immensity is one of the most necessary things for our world at this time. For one thing, when people begin to realize that God is the God of the heavens, they may think twice about trying to twist him round their little fingers. And they may, on the other hand, begin to feel a little more confident about the world situation—when they get a glimpse of God's immensity as revealed in the immensity of the heavens.

Day after Day

One of the most boring things you can do is fly the Atlantic for about the thirtieth time. You may take off from the American side of the ocean late in the evening and wait about an hour and a half for something to eat while the drinks are being served. Then you eat your meal and start dozing.

The movie comes on, and the captain announces that it is now 3:00 a.m., Greenwich Mean Time. The people next to you climb over you to pay their third visit to the rear of the aircraft, and you wait for them to return. The cabin gets cool, so you hunt for a blanket and snooze fitfully until you give up and try to read. But your eyes feel as if they are full of sand, so you decide to go for a walk to the only place there is to go, only to discover that everyone else on the plane is asleep.

One thing on the trip makes all this tedium almost

worthwhile: the dawn is gorgeous. Slowly the blackness begins to pale, and a succession of pastel colors acts as an overture to the sunrise. That's one lovely thing to anticipate.

It's comforting to know that sunrise will come right on time. We reckon on it and even talk about the certainty of it: "As sure as day follows the night." That's what David means when he speaks of *"day after day"* in verse 2. The fact that the days come and go with total consistency and reliability says something about God's fidelity and reliability. That is something else we need to know in today's unstable world. We need to be reassured that the God of immensity is also the God of fidelity.

THE BEAUTY OF THE SUN

"In the heavens he has pitched a tent for the sun, which is like a bridegroom coming forth from his pavilion, like a champion rejoicing to run his course. It rises at one end of the heavens, and makes its circuit to the other; nothing is hidden from its heat." (vv. 4c–6)

The psalmist's description of the sun is so beautiful that I feel reluctant to comment. Allow me to point out, however, two things on David's mind.

First, he thinks of the freshness and exuberance of the daily sunrise and says it reminds him of a bridegroom on his wedding day. (As a pastor who has officiated at many weddings, I must say that my experience of bridegrooms has not always been so positive! But that's not important.)

Second, the sun is relentless in moving through its circuit, touching to a greater or lesser extent all the ends of the earth. What a picture of radiant, irresistible, benevolent majesty, and how easy it is to apply this revelation to the being of God. These are some of the things the heavens say to those who take time to listen to their silent message.

Before we go further, let's pause to consider the thrust of the psalm so far. The heavens declare in no uncertain terms the glory, immensity, fidelity, and majesty of God. They say it silently but eloquently. And they proclaim it to the ends of the earth.

But something is missing in this revelation. The picture of God we now have is remote and vast and vaguely disturbing. Is that all that God is willing to reveal of himself? If so, a person might also prefer not to know rather than be tantalized with such a frustrating partial view of God. The sheer unapproachableness and otherworldliness of God as he is revealed in the heavens does little to warm the heart of the observer and does even less to allay his fears and instruct his mind. Man needs a further revelation.

REVELATION IN THE WORD

"The law of the LORD is perfect, reviving the soul. The statutes of the LORD are trustworthy, making wise the simple. The precepts of the LORD are right, giving joy to the heart. The commands of the LORD are radiant, giving light to the eyes. The fear of the LORD is pure, enduring forever. The ordinances of the LORD are sure and altogether righteous." (vv. 7–9)

In addition to speaking to us through creation, God speaks to us through Scripture. This is a far more detailed voice than that of creation. It speaks in specific terms, whereas creation deals only in generalities. Indeed, without the voice of Scripture, much of creation would be a complete enigma to us; but when both voices speak, they reveal the mysteries of God and earth with great clarity.

Here is a different approach to the search for knowledge than the route of speculative philosophy. Revelation can clarify, where speculation may only mystify. One of modern society's great needs is to turn once more to the revelation of God for answers rather than lean upon human speculation.

At this point we must say a fond but firm farewell to much of human philosophy, for human thinking and scriptural truth seldom agree. Accordingly, people have to decide which of these they will listen to, and on which of these they will build their lives.

Scriptural truth has fallen on deaf ears in most areas of contemporary society. Much of what people think today about the mysteries of life comes not from God and his scriptural revelation, but from humans and their limited and often erroneous speculation. To put it bluntly, we have an awful lot of dangerous nonsense filling the areas of people's minds that were intended for the truth of God as revealed in Scripture.

Without belaboring the point, let me offer one example. There is so much thinking today on the subject of rights. Many of society's problems at this time appear to be caused by people's rights being abused. As a result, we are almost totally rights oriented. The Scriptures, however, speak far more about responsibilities than about rights. According to Scripture, if people concentrated on their responsibilities, others would have their rights.

But in all honesty, do you think there will ever come a day when people will stop insisting on their rights and start attending to their responsibilities? I have tried this theory on a number of people, and they all look at me with a degree of incredulity. "You've gotta be kidding," they say. Yet I insist that unless we return to scriptural principles and throw out much that is the product of humanistic thought, we have our course set straight for societal shipwreck.

Here's another example of revelation needing the truth of Scripture. On warm Sunday mornings when the golf course beckons, there is sometimes a conflict as to where people will look for divine revelation. "I can worship God on the golf course as readily as in church," some say.

I for one do not dispute that. I simply ask, "Do you?"

The fact of the matter is that in a good church one will hear the Word of God proclaimed, but there is little chance of that at even the best-equipped country club!

Suppose that a worshiper on the golf course worshiped the God that he saw revealed in greens and sand traps. Do you realize that he would never learn from that worship experience that his soul can be converted? The golf course doesn't display that information on the tees or print it on the backs of scorecards. The only place to learn of the gospel is in the Word of God, and nowhere else.

Making Wise the Simple

David says that God's Word is able to make "wise the simple" (v. 7). We need to make a clear distinction between knowledge and wisdom. Knowledge is the amassing of facts. Wisdom is knowing what on earth to do with the facts we have amassed. This distinction can help us understand why some remarkable, erudite people are in such quandaries and why some relatively ignorant people have peace of mind and demonstrate integrated living.

The Scriptures make simple people wise to what they should do with their knowledge. The principle is "The fear of the LORD is the beginning of wisdom" (Psalm 111:10). Only Scripture insists on that point.

A knowledge of high finance may enable a man to make a fortune by age thirty, but in the making of it he may unmake his family, his health, and his integrity. If somehow this brilliant man could have gotten some wisdom along with his knowledge, he might have acknowledged the Lord in his family relations, in his use of time and energy, and in his moral principles. But to do so he would need to act on the basis of sound scriptural truth rather than the principles of everyday business ethics.

Rejoicing the Heart

God's revealed will can also bring *"joy to the heart"* (v. 8). In the first chapter of this book, we talked about the pursuit of happiness, and there is no need to say again what was said there. But remember that the way to happiness as revealed in Scripture is not heavily traveled. The biblical approach is written off by the majority of our fellow travelers as antiquated and Victorian, without holding anything remotely attractive to them.

Giving Light to the Eyes

Knowledge of God's Word can also *"give light to our eyes"* (v. 8). Have you ever seen children at their first birthday party? Remember how their eyes got as big as saucers when they saw the cake with its one proud candle? Can you remember the wonder of it all, the sheer thrill of the little child? Their eyes were opened to something new and strange and totally captivating. I remember meeting a man with a PhD who had just discovered the Bible. He had the same look of wonder on his face as the child with that first birthday cake. He kept saying, "I didn't know that. I didn't know that." In fact, he hadn't known much, though he was about as "educated" as one can get. What a difference the revelation of God made on his life!

We have described only some of the things that exposure to the Word of God produces in lives. And remember that these things do not come from speculation, and only partially from the revelation of creation. It's the law of the Lord that does the trick.

This psalm describes the Scriptures not only as the law of God but also as *"statutes," "precepts," "commands,"* and *"ordinances"* (vv. 7–9). These terms have an authoritative ring to them that must not be overlooked. When God speaks in Scripture, he says what needs to be said, and he really means what he says.

He Really Means It!

In many areas of society, people are looking for an authoritative leader with an authoritative voice who can tell them what to do and how to do it. In fact, we live in such a turbulent age that, if someone can dream up a wild enough idea and project it with enough confidence, he almost seems guaranteed a following. Deep in the human heart, there is a great need for clear direction.

The Scriptures provide us direction without equivocation. But this in itself poses a problem because most human beings are a bundle of contradictions. They want an authoritative statement, just so long as it tells them with authority that it is okay to do whatever they intended to do anyway! Like the church that was looking for a pastor who would in a fearless, forthright, and uncompromising manner tell them just what they wanted to hear!

God does not work that way. He spells things out, explains what not to do, and how to do it or not do it. He then promises what will happen if we do or don't obey what he says. And then he leaves the choice to us. Whether you feel inclined to obey or disinclined to obey, you can be equally sure of what will happen, for God has spoken.

What lovely words are used to describe the authoritative statements of Scripture. *"The fear of the LORD is pure. . . . The ordinances of the LORD are sure"* (v. 9). The assurance of Scripture's power and validity is the greatest possible incentive to obedience. That assurance, more than anything else, stimulates the desire to depend upon God's promises.

Just to know that you will be doing the *right* thing is a wonderful feeling indeed. To be convinced that you are being told the sure, pure truth is more comforting than words can tell. It makes a person respond with great joy and confidence.

THE SWEETNESS OF GOD'S WORD

"They are more precious than gold,
than much pure gold; they are sweeter than honey,
than honey from the comb." (v. 10)

The first time I ate a mango was an unforgettable moment. I had been told by my Jamaican friends that the only way to eat a mango was to stand up to your neck in the Caribbean. I was not particularly impressed by my first sight of a mango, but the feel of the Caribbean was just what I needed. So I waded out in the unbelievably warm water and was duly given a dry-looking piece of fruit, most unappetizing in appearance. I watched how my friends got into it, did the same thing, and, oh, the bliss! It was just about the sweetest thing I had ever tasted. I could easily become a mango-holic.

Have you ever gotten into the dry, dull pages of Scripture and then tasted their sweetness? Have you come to its pages with fear and found sweet peace? Have you come with guilt and found sweet forgiveness? This is the beauty of God's Word. It is "sweeter than honey." If you obey it and believe it, then that which is authoritative becomes attractive. Fight and resist it, and it becomes unbelievably bitter.

SOME WARNINGS AND REWARDS

"By them is your servant warned; in keeping them there is great reward." (v. 11)

The strange and wonderful book that God has given us is not only authoritative; it also at times manages to be abrasive. God warns his followers through his Word and rewards those who keep his statutes. This is straight talking, and there is no doubt that Scripture is a little too hot for some to handle. But there's one thing to remember about abrasive materials. If you let them rub with the grain, they smooth things out, but if you rub against the grain, they rough things up. It all depends on the reaction of the material being abraded!

This leads us to the final section of the psalm (vv. 12–14), in which David shows something of the response of his own heart to the truths God has revealed to him.

GOD'S WORD IS A MIRROR

"Who can discern his errors? Forgive my hidden faults. Keep your servant also from willful sins; may they not rule over me. . . . May the words of my mouth and the meditation of my heart be pleasing in your sight, O LORD, my Rock and my Redeemer." (vv. 12–14)

The Word of God functions in many ways in our lives. Sometimes it comes on like a trumpet; other times it hits like a hammer. Sometimes it is like a seed, quietly growing in the soil of the hearer's heart.

As he comes to the conclusion of this psalm, David sees the Scripture as a mirror. The Word of God has made him conscious of his own errors of judgment and action. He seeks forgiveness. He has also seen the cover stripped away from his *"hidden faults."* He wants to be cleansed of this kind of behavior.

David has also been made painfully aware that some of his living has been downright disobedience. He calls it *"willful"* sin, and he desires to be freed from the tyranny he experiences in this area.

This is the kind of response God expects from the person who hears his Word and allows it to sink deep into his or her heart. It is a totally different response from that of the person who is still working on the basis of speculation.

The "speculator" tends to operate on procedures that seem right. If they don't work out, he or she speculates again and comes up with something else—that also doesn't work. That approach is as unsatisfactory as a referee changing rules halfway through a game instead of sticking with the rules and enforcing them. Rules enforced lead to a completed game. Rules ignored or changed lead to chaos.

One of life's greatest challenges is living according to what God has said, instead of vacillating around what various of our fellow humans have thought. Living by what God has said leads to a reevaluation of the words that come from our lips, and even a careful look at the very thoughts that churn in our mind. And the real push comes when, having taken note of these things, we say with David, *"May the words of my mouth and the meditation of my heart be pleasing in your sight, O LORD."*

Instead of a variety of theories emanating from a host of philosophies that breed inevitable conflicts of thought and ideology, this approach leads to a great unity of purpose: the desire to please God according to his revealed will. There's hope in this approach; there's none in the other.

Psalm 23

1 The LORD is my shepherd, I shall not be in want.
2 He makes me lie down in green pastures,
he leads me beside quiet waters,
3 he restores my soul.
He guides me in paths of righteousness
for his name's sake.
4 Even though I walk
through the valley of the shadow of death,
I will fear no evil,
for you are with me;
your rod and your staff,
they comfort me.

5 You prepare a table before me
in the presence of my enemies.
You anoint my head with oil;
my cup overflows.
6 Surely goodness and love will follow me
all the days of my life,
and I will dwell in the house of the LORD
forever.

WHEN YOU DON'T KNOW
WHO OR WHAT YOU ARE

I know a woman who has spent years concentrating on the fact that she is a failure. According to her, everything she has ever tried has failed, and there is no possibility of her ever being able to succeed at anything. She has made a number of attempts at suicide and has even failed in these. Her children are suffering, her husband is suffering, her marriage has suffered, and just about everything has fallen apart because of her poor self-image.

On the other hand, there are people who seem to have inflated self-images that leave others almost gasping in disbelief. Robert Burns, the Scottish poet, mused,

> Oh wad some Pow'r the giftie gie us
> To see oursels as ithers see us!

That way of thinking is healthy. One of the best antidotes to a faulty self-image is to listen to what other people say about you. But there is something even more valuable than what the famous poet Burns suggests. It is to be able to see yourself as God sees you. In fact, the only

really adequate self-image comes from an acceptance of the divine evaluation of our lives.

Fortunately, God has not been at all reticent in this area. The ironic thing about God's evaluation of people is that he appears to go right along with what the extremists say on both sides of the self-image argument. Some passages of Scripture imply that we should consider ourselves as the woman who failed at even suicide. Other Scripture statements describe people as if the ultimate victory is theirs and absolutely nothing can stop them. So what is the balanced view? Where is the truth about self-image to be found?

WE HAVE A SHEPHERD

"The LORD is my shepherd, I shall not be in want." (v. 1)

Perhaps this best known of all psalms has some answers to this problem. This psalm is the testimony of one who needed and found a shepherd. Careful study reveals that the writer was perfectly thrilled with the Shepherd he had discovered and was thoroughly enjoying his relationship with this Shepherd.

Presumably, therefore, the writer of Psalm 23 felt like a sheep in many ways, and in his capacity as a sheep was finding some real answers in the Shepherd. This is the first clue to a healthy self-image: the sheep image! After all, other Bible passages describe us as sheep—for instance, "We all, like sheep, have gone astray, each of us has turned to his own way" (Isaiah 53:6).

I have no expert knowledge of sheep, but I have had considerable experiential knowledge of them. I was brought up in a part of England known for its sheep raising. In fact, they say that people don't die in those parts; they just turn into sheep! That I doubt, but I do not doubt that it would be hard to find more stupid animals than sheep.

Wandering Sheep

For some reason, sheep have a remarkable aptitude for getting lost. They can be perfectly at home in a pleasant pasture, until one revolutionary spirit among them finds a hole in the fence. In less time than it takes to tell it, they will desert the grass and head for the hole. In five minutes flat there won't be a sheep in the pasture, and there will be hundreds on the road. Honking horns, bleating lambs, screeching tires, baaing ewes turn the quiet countryside into bedlam. All because some sheep decided to go astray, leading many others after it.

Now, any sensible sheep would survey such chaos and say, "Baaaaaaa—it was better in the pasture. Let's go back again." Does that ever happen? No way. The sheep will mess around, creating more and more chaos, until a dog arrives. Then they will all head off in the opposite direction from the dog, regardless of where that might lead them!

There is something vaguely disturbing about sheep behavior, especially as it relates to human behavior.

94

People do have an inherited tendency to desert what is good for them, believing that something better is just out of reach. To them "the grass is always greener on the other side of the fence." Herd instinct is just a polite expression for what turns out to be flock folly! We head after strong leaders with great enthusiasm, rarely stopping to check *where* they are leading us. In every human being is an inbred propensity to go wrong, and failure to admit this must inevitably lead to an inaccurate self-image.

Scripture is full of illustrations of this point. Many great figures of the faith had this in common: they recognized their own inbuilt bias to sin, their disturbing ability to go wrong. Some of them have their failures recorded in frightening detail: David, Saul, Moses, Peter, Paul, John Mark. And this is no accident. These things are recorded for our benefit, for unless we come to terms with our own failure, rebellion, and sin (the sheep syndrome), we will never have a realistic and accurate self-image.

Helpless or Invincible?

The other side of the coin is that any sheep who goes about things God's way can have a self-image that allows it to say things such as, "I shall not be in want. . . . I will fear no evil. . . . my cup overflows" (vv. 1, 4, 5). This is the language of a confident, outgoing, almost exuberantly aggressive person. But this is exactly what the Lord Jesus talked about later when he told his unsuspecting disciples, "I am sending you out like sheep among wolves" (Matthew 10:16).

At first this appears to be totally contradictory. If I am to think of myself as a sheep, how can I think I will be strong enough to frighten wolves? On the other hand, if I can frighten wolves, why pretend I'm a sheep? Am I a sheep, or am I a wolf frightener? Am I a helpless, hopeless failure, or am I invincible?

Rather than wrestle with this problem, many people decide to settle for one or the other. But the truth is we do not have the privilege of deciding either/or. The real picture is in being both.

The Sheep-Shepherd Relationship

Sheep with shepherds and sheep without shepherds are totally different. It's the shepherd who makes the difference. The Lord Jesus is the Good Shepherd, who not only gives his life for the sheep but also knows them, calls them by name, and leads them (see John 10).

When an adequate relationship exists between sheep who freely admit their need of shepherding and the Shepherd who cares and leads in love and wisdom, the sheep begin to demonstrate great qualities not previously apparent. They never pretend to be anything more or less than sheep, but they never settle for a lifestyle that is less than what the shepherd would want for them.

The simple phrase *"The LORD is my shepherd"* says it all. Note carefully the one of whom the psalmist speaks: the

Lord. We are familiar by now with all that this name implies. Never forget that this remarkable Lord has accepted responsibility to act as Shepherd for insignificant human individuals. This is a sure and certain promise. To believe this does more for the fractured self-image than anything else that I know.

The relationship between sheep and Shepherd is very personal, as emphasized by the word *my*. It can't get any more intimate than that. Some people talk about God in generalities but are reluctant to get personal about him. To say that Christ is real and relevant to them personally is more than they can manage. To profess intimacy with him is to them the gravest embarrassment. But God looks for as personal a commitment from us, as he offers to us.

The absolute certainty of the whole relationship is found in one tiny word right in the middle of the statement: "*The* LORD *is my shepherd.*" No "ifs" or "buts," just a clear "is." Put it all together and you have the kind of conviction that makes sheep into wolf chasers, mice into men, an inadequate person into an adequate person.

CONTENT IN GREEN PASTURES

"He makes me lie down in green pastures . . ." (v. 2a)

In all probability, you have never had an uncontrollable urge to make a sheep lie down. Just in case this should happen to you, let me save you some trouble. Sheep are such anatomical oddities that the only way to their haunches is through their stomachs. In other words, you can't make a hungry sheep lie down. But if you can fill its stomach, it will find a quiet place, lie down, and contentedly ruminate on how good things are under the shepherd's control. *Contentment* is the word we must emphasize at this point, for contentment is a missing ingredient in our society. We live in a discontented age.

There is such frightening pressure on people to prove themselves. The demands of our society are such that, in order to be acceptable, many people are about to destroy themselves in the feverish acquisition of status symbols and the like. And when these things are acquired, their preservation appears to demand almost as much time and energy and often produces as many phobias and ulcers as their acquisition.

But what bliss to be content! To have no overwhelming desire to prove anything. To be able to look the world in the eye and say, "World, look at me! I'm simply a sheep who is content to be all that, and only what, the Shepherd wants me to be. Take me or leave me. I'm nothing more than this. I have no desire to try to fulfill all of society's lofty expectations of me. I have little interest in amassing all the things that society says are necessary for my well-being. I'm content."

STILL WATERS IN STORMS

". . . he leads me beside quiet waters . . ." (v. 2b)

Under stormy waves are deeper quiet waters. That is where the fish live. A few years ago I went scuba diving in a fabulous coral reef. The small boat that took us out was tossed like a cork on the choppy sea, but once we got under the surface the silence was deafening. Green light filtered through banks of multicolored coral. Ridiculously shaped fish swam past us with utter disinterest, and in the weightlessness of the quiet, deep water we swam and relaxed.

Many of our storms are self-made. In the mad, crazy desire to be something that we are not or to compensate for what we'll never be, we sail into all kinds of choppy waters. But there is an alternative; it is to allow the Shepherd to lead into the places of quiet and peace. Given the chance, he will.

This is not to suggest that all storms are self-made. Innumerable situations for which we cannot be held responsible may hit us with the force of a southwesterly gale. Nevertheless, the principle is the same: even in these storms, God is committed to lead us into peaceful waters—even while the storm continues to rage.

WE ALL NEED RESTORING

". . . he restores my soul." (v. 3a)

I know that you're probably thinking, *All this peace and contentment business is all right, but it just doesn't work out that way. In fact, that kind of talk only makes me feel guiltier that I'm not that way.*

I'm glad you thought that, because I agree with you! Obviously, you are going to have moments when you feel that the roof has fallen in on you, and it will take all you have to survive. You reserve the right once in a while to come apart at the seams! And even if you don't admit such a possibility, you will come apart from time to time anyway. The Lord allows for this and restores your soul.

Some time ago a young man came to see me. He was doing a paper for his communications class at the university, and he had chosen to use my ministry as the basis of his project. He arrived in my study at the end of a day in which I had written a chapter of this book, prepared a sermon outline, done two TV shows, counseled two or three people, met with the missions committee, and I forget what else. Grinning, he stretched out his hand and said, "How're you doing, Pastor?"

"Pooped," I replied.

His smile froze.

When we had concluded our business, he said an interesting thing: "Thank you for letting me see that you get tired. I thought you didn't have that kind of problem." That was very gracious of him, but he obviously hadn't been thinking too clearly. Of course I get tired and discouraged, weary, worn, and sad, but I don't have to stay that way. The Lord "*restores my soul.*"

WALKING THE RIGHT PATH

*"He guides me in paths of righteousness
for his name's sake."* (v. 3b–c)

Fear of making a wrong move paralyzes many people. I am constantly asked to counsel with those who, in reality, want me to make up their minds for them. They are so anxious about making the right decision, and so unsure of their own ability to discern the way to go, that they try to put the responsibility on other shoulders.

I firmly believe that counsel and advice should be readily shared among those who wish to do the right thing, but something important must be stressed at this point. *"He guides me in the paths of righteousness for his name's sake."* The Lord is concerned that his sheep go the right way—for *his* name's sake. In fact, he is more concerned that his sheep go the right way than they can ever be! So he is prepared to make the way clear to the unsure and to direct those who will accept his direction.

This takes much of the stress out of living because if the Lord has promised to lead in the path of his choice, the most important thing the sheep has to do is maintain a right attitude of *fellowship*, which will guarantee the blessing of God's *leadership* no matter what comes along. I have experienced numerous occasions in my life when I had no idea what I was getting into, but there was always quiet confidence that I was heading in the right direction—not because I claim infallibility, but because at the time in question I knew I was trusting the Lord Jesus Christ to make the right path open to me.

It may sound as if this approach would destroy human insight and decisiveness. This is not the case. The one who follows the Lord will need to exercise all of his or her human faculties and act in dependence on God as well. So check out your options, evaluate your decisions, get all the advice you can, explore the consequences, and then, in dependence on the Shepherd to stop you if you're wrong, go ahead.

NOT ALONE IN THE VALLEY

"Even though I walk through the valley of the shadow of death, I will fear no evil, for you are with me. . . ."
(v. 4a–d)

Some people have a terrible fear of death. Others fear dying. Most fear both. Some fear neither death nor dying. Sheep seem to fit into this latter category. There is, of course, considerable trepidation in all our lives when we are faced with the unknown. And death is certainly unknown to all of us from an experiential point of view. So apprehension is perfectly understandable and permissible, but stark fear is not. The reason is plain to see: *"you are with me."*

The One who is with the Christian in death and dying is the One who has been there already and has always come through with flying colors: the risen Lord. If it is true, therefore, that the "last enemy" is death, it is great news indeed to know that the One who has blown death wide open in resurrection is "with me" at all times, no matter what difficult circumstances life may bring my way.

I am not suggesting that the person who believes this should do anything to precipitate his or her own demise, either by his or her own hand or by lack of care. I do find, however, that this kind of fearlessness, this attitude of resting in the Lord, is magnificent to behold. It may thrust believers out to work in the trouble spots of the world with equanimity. It may lead them to work in difficult areas that others shun and avoid at all costs. It will certainly equip them to meet the frightening situations of modern living with considerably more composure than the average person is able to muster.

Such people have a firm conviction, you see, that the Lord *of* the valley will take them *through* the valley. Then, when the Lord decides it's time to go, Christians can go with joy—right on time!

POKING AND PRODDING

". . . your rod and your staff, they comfort me." (v. 4e–f)

The shepherd's equipment was unsophisticated. Just a rod and a staff. But they were all that he needed. They were applied with two things in mind: protection and correction. When marauding animals came along, the shepherd would whack them with the rod. When the wandering sheep fell over a cliff, the staff would pull them back to safety. When they needed a poke, they would get it from the rod or the staff.

All this poking and prodding and whacking doesn't sound too appealing, does it? To the sheep it is. *"Your rod and your staff, they comfort me."* It's a joy to know that you are protected and will be corrected as the need arises. Protected from the dangers that will come upon you unaware. Corrected when you do things that will unnecessarily get you into trouble.

Some people can't stand to be corrected, and they are hard to live with. They impose their views and ideas with such vehemence that it is quite clear they are unsure of themselves and their arguments. But when people are open to the rebuke of the Lord, however administered, they become much more balanced and amenable.

PROTECTED AND UNPERTURBED

"You prepare a table before me in the presence of my enemies." (v. 5a–b)

I get the wildest picture in my mind when I read verse 5 of this psalm. The old sheep is seated at a sumptuous sheep feast. The table is laden with all that a sheep could ever wish to eat. All around are wolves, licking their chops, growling and yapping. The sheep, however, is quite unperturbed. "Don't bother me; can't you see I'm busy?"

The ability to keep one's cool in a stressful situation is a delightful trait that appears to be the gift of an ever-decreasing minority. In fact, we men almost seem to think we have to blow our fuses to assert our masculinity. Or we have to yell and wave our fists to let people know how important we are. But imperturbability—that calm composure under the constant stress of life—is a joy to practice and behold.

Next time you stand in line for a plane ticket on a Monday morning with all the ruffled business travelers, don't join them in hassling the poor ticket agent at the counter. Try telling your "enemies" of impatience, arrogance, and selfishness to go away because you're busy resting in the Lord, who is bigger than a ticket counter and greater than a hectic airline schedule. You could even try commending the agent for doing an impossible job well.

ANOINTED AND OVERFLOWING

"You anoint my head with oil; my cup overflows." (v. 5c–d)

Sheep do get their heads bruised and their wool ripped at times. But they don't have to display their injuries to everyone. Neither do they have to sulk in a corner, licking their wounds. They can have the oil of anointing and healing poured in by the Lord in overflowing measure.

In the business world there are numerous occasions when heads get butted and wool gets torn. Fragile egos are shattered, careers go to the wall, reputations are shredded. But it doesn't have to be that way. Go to the One who dispenses the oil of anointing. God knows, cares, and understands perfectly. A few moments in the quiet place with the Shepherd can save limitless hours in the office with the boss or on the couch with the psychiatrist.

GOODNESS AND LOVE ALWAYS

"Surely goodness and love will follow me all the days of my life, and I will dwell in the house of the LORD forever." (v. 6)

There are only two things that we have to learn in this life: how to live and how to die! I think the author of Psalm 23 has learned both. As for life, the clear testimony of the writer is that all the days of his life he will experience the goodness and mercy of God. And when death comes along, he *"will dwell in the house of the LORD forever."* That sums it all up!

In closing, let's just take a moment to look at our own self-image. Can we freely admit our sheeplike capacity for going wrong and gladly acknowledge our dependence on God to lead and provide? If so, then we can look at life and death with confidence and equanimity, knowing that we honestly have nothing to prove. In the Lord, we lack nothing at all. As our Shepherd, he will provide all our needs willingly and lovingly as we follow his paths of righteousness.

Psalm 27

1 The LORD is my light and my salvation—
whom shall I fear?
The LORD is the stronghold of my life—
of whom shall I be afraid?
2 When evil men advance against me
to devour my flesh,
when all my enemies and my foes attack me,
they will stumble and fall.
3 Though an army besiege me,
my heart will not fear;
though war break out against me,
even then will I be confident.

....

13 I am still confident of this:
I will see the goodness of the LORD
in the land of the living.
14 Wait for the LORD;
be strong and take heart
and wait for the LORD.

CHAPTER SEVEN

WHEN FEAR COMES CALLING
AND WON'T GO AWAY

You are alone at home. You think you hear something—or someone—downstairs. Icy fingers grip your insides; your mind freezes. Fear has immobilized you.

Or it's your turn to stand up and say something. The person ahead of you has done a superb job, and you know you can't match her performance. Your heart beats fast; your knees turn to rubber. Fear has gotten hold of you.

The phone rings at 1:00 a.m. Your teenagers are at the first party you have allowed them to attend. There's been an accident, you think, and your hand just won't reach for that phone. Fear has paralyzed you.

You're in a room full of people. Everybody is enjoying the event, except you. Nobody knows you and you don't know them. You would like to be included, but you hesitate to break into a group's conversations. You vow to yourself, *Never again*. Fear has isolated you.

THE ANTIDOTE TO FEAR

"The LORD is my light and my salvation. . . . The LORD is the stronghold of my life . . ." (v. 1a, c)

Fear can become a totally controlling influence in our lives. It is common knowledge that the majority of people in hospitals around the Western world are there not because of physical illness, but because of illness of the mind. And one of the main contributing factors to psychological disturbance and emotional sickness is fear.

David, the psalmist, had no training in psychology, but he had a lot of real-life experience with fear! And he had a lot of faith! So his psalm has a wealth of sound principles and personal testimony, even if it lacks technical psychological terminology.

Personally, I welcome this, for while I have the profoundest respect for those who have studied the intricacies of the human psyche and can deal with its involved imbalances, I also believe that the Word of God has illustrations and principles that can bring untold blessings to the fearful and the anxious.

David's problem was that he had been run off his throne, the victim of a conspiracy from within his own family. (Note: Bible students do not agree in identifying this psalm with a particular event in David's life. But many believe it relates to the time of Absalom's rebellion, and that is the assumption here.) David had gone into hiding and was in desperate straits. He had set up a government-in-exile at Mahanaim, across Jordan, and had organized his loyalist forces to meet the expected onslaught from his son Absalom (2 Samuel 15–17).

Absalom, in the meantime, had gathered all the outstanding young men to his cause, had publicly disgraced his father, the king, and was preparing a great army to finish David off. Humiliated, outgunned, and heavily outnumbered by his enemies, David certainly knew fear. But he also had some great things to say about how to handle it. And they all involved trusting the Lord.

The Lord As Light

The small town where I was born, in the northwest corner of England, was famous for its rich seam of iron ore. For years the iron had been mined, and there were many deserted mine shafts and tunnels around the town. In the fall these deserted areas were suddenly alive with people picking the blackberries that grew there in profusion.

When blackberry-picking season came to an end, the spirit of exploration took over. I have vivid recollections of following rusty railroad tracks through wild landscape, entertaining all types of adventurous thoughts in my young mind. One day I strode manfully into a deserted tunnel and very quickly found myself in the dark. Striding manfully quickly changed to thinking childishly, and I was just about to panic until I saw a light at the end of the tunnel. The fear went, and I quickly regained my manly stride.

For many of us the future is like a long, dark tunnel, and like all tunnels of that nature, it is a little scary. However, there is a light at the end of the tunnel. In fact, this light is so bright that it shines right into the tunnel.

The light I refer to is the same one of whom David spoke: *"The LORD is my light."*

The future can be divided into two parts: the future that lies ahead of us up to the grave, and the future that stretches beyond the grave. God sheds great light on both. He is the one who alone can give "grace to help in time of need" (Hebrews 4:16 KJV). This is the light he sheds before us for every day of our lives. At every time of need, he promises to give us the ability to handle it. To believe this and to live in the good of it is to banish the darkness and to flood the future with light.

The old adage says it best: "I don't know what the future holds, but I know who holds the future." Countless illustrations of this come to mind, both from my personal experience and from my contacts with hundreds of people who have found it to be true.

Then there is the matter of death and what lies beyond. As we have already seen, fear relating to death and dying is extremely common. But Jesus said, "I am the resurrection and the life. Those whose believe in me, even though they die like everyone else, will live again" (John 11:25 NLT). The Lord Jesus gives to all who trust him the assurance that when they have him they also have eternal life.

The believing heart responds to this kind of assurance with great joy and confidence. The believer has so much light banishing the darkness of uncertainty that he or she may well become as outspoken as Paul and shout, "Where O death, is your victory? Where, O death, is your sting?"

WHAT WORKS WHEN LIFE DOESN'T

(1 Corinthians 15:55). When a person comes to the realization that the Lord is the light of his or her life, fear of the future dissipates quickly.

The Lord As Savior

Guilt can play havoc with a person's life. When fear of disclosure is added to the guilt, extreme misery can result. Unless the person finds some deep-down answers to the guilt and fear, his or her well-being may be jeopardized.

So are there any deep-down answers to this problem of guilt and fear? All sin is against God, and unless it is viewed in this perspective, no adequate answer for guilt can be discovered. I am aware that many counselors would strongly disagree with this statement. I insist on it, nevertheless, for this reason: when we begin to see that God has laid down standards of behavior for which we are unanswerable to him, we can understand how desperately important our actions really are. Actually, this ought to be an encouragement, for most of us need some kind of reassurance from time to time that we are important. When we see that our actions, important as they are, have been out of order according to God's judgment, we can see that we are in serious trouble in our relationships with him

There is, however, a glorious side to this whole situation. The God to whom we are responsible and against whom we have sinned is ready, willing, and able to forgive us. The depth of his forgiveness is so great that he is free to declare us "not guilty" in the highest court of heaven. This forgiveness has come because on the cross Christ has paid the penalty for all our sins, allowing God to be perfectly justified in granting us forgiveness.

If we see ourselves as sinners in need of God's forgiveness, and then hear that Christ had died for this very purpose, we can begin to get excited about being forgiven. The language we can use to express this excitement may be something like *"The LORD is my light and my salvation."*

Understanding that the Lord is *Savior* helps us to grasp the greatness of being forgiven. And that realization leads to freedom of expression about our past life. When God has forgiven a person, a great openness about being forgiven results.

I know a young woman who, when she was in school, worked in a women's fashion store. Unable to resist the temptation of the beautiful clothes, she began to steal them. Eventually, she became so fearful and ashamed that she confessed her sin to the Lord and sought his forgiveness. She then told her employer and asked for an opportunity to repay him. The employer was so moved by her repentance and desire to do the right thing that he helped her greatly.

When she told this story in our church, she concluded in a way that I will never forget. Throwing her arms in the air in a great gesture of freedom, she said, "Any of you can look in any part of my life and there will be nothing hidden. All is confessed; all is forgiven. It's great to be free."

This is the kind of freedom from fear so many people

are seeking. It comes only from a sense of the saving, forgiving power of Christ in a life.

The Lord As Our Stronghold

The terrible sense of inadequacy that so many people live
with makes them dread the day-to-day situations they
must face. It is hard to imagine how some are able to face
daily challenges that they know they cannot meet.
Sometimes it is their own fault. Their egos will not allow
them to admit their own limitations, so they are driven to
live in realms where they don't belong, striving to be
people they will never be.

But this is not the case with everyone. Some are where
they belong but don't feel they can do what is expected of
them. New mothers, new husbands, new recruits all have
the same fears. Tired salespeople, injured athletes, fading
beauties know the same gnawing uncertainties.

What should people do in such situations? First, they
should find out what the Lord wants them to be and do.
Then they should see if what they want differs from his
plans for them. Having cleared this up in their own
minds, they must decide which way they intend to go. If
they decide to make a commitment to be what God wants
them to be, they can be sure of one thing: he will equip
them to do it.

A word of caution may be necessary at this point: God
does not promise to make fading beauties stop fading or

to make hurting athletes stop hurting. He may be trying to tell the respective beauty or athlete, by their very experience, that he has something else in mind for them. But he does promise to show us what he has in mind. Then, when we go along with him, he works on our behalf.

This makes people rejoice amid their busy lives. As they battle with the everyday details of work and responsibility, they can say, *"The LORD is the stronghold of my life."*

The joy of this kind of dependence banishes all fear because the load of responsibility is on the Lord to provide the strength. And he never fails.

NO FEAR

". . . whom shall I fear? . . . of whom shall I be afraid?
Though an army besiege me, my heart will not fear;
though war break out against me,
even then will I be confident." (v. 1b, d; 3)

Having made known his absolute confidence in God, David asks the resounding question *"Whom shall I fear?"* and then follows right through with *"Of whom shall I be afraid?"* Who could possibly dare to answer David's question, in the light of his steadfast faith! In fact, it is impossible to think of anyone who could frighten him or any circumstance that could unnerve him, since the Lord is his light, his strength, and his salvation.

As if to drive the point home, David recounts the ways

in which he has seen his enemies fall all over themselves as they came up against him. He goes so far as to say that even if he finds himself surrounded and overwhelmingly outnumbered, *"even then I will be confident"* (v. 3).

What Causes Fear?

People get frightened for many different reasons. People have differing personalities, and some appear to be more susceptible to fear than others. The Greek doctors of old held some interesting theories. They believed that personality was determined by the fluids that sloshed around in people's bodies. As silly as this may seem, we still carry some of their thinking into our day by using the terms they coined. *Phlegmatic* (excess phlegm), *sanguine* (excess blood), *choleric* (excess yellow bile), and *melancholic* (excess black bile) are expressions with which we are familiar when referring to personality types.

Some of these personality types seem more or less prone to fear than others, and there is no doubt that sometimes we attribute our fear or lack of it to our temperaments. However, this can be a dangerous oversimplification because everybody is afraid of something and sooner or later will show it. Temperament does play a part, but only in terms of the things that frighten us, not in terms of whether or not we are ever afraid.

The bully who attacks an elderly woman may, in actual fact, be more fearful than she is. He may discover his own fears when he feels the sharp edge of her tongue and gets the point of her umbrella.

Various traumatic events can take place in our lives and leave deep scars for years. Some people nearly drown in childhood and for the rest of their lives have a mortal dread of water. (Most small boys have this dread, without nearly drowning!) The man who is bitten by a dog may act on the principle of "once bitten, twice shy" for the rest of his life.

The determinists among us are convinced that we are what we are because of the environments in which we live. Everything is determined by circumstances outside our control. This is a gross exaggeration, but like most exaggerations, it contains an element of truth. The boy who was raised by a domineering dad who ridiculed him every time he opened his mouth may well grow up to have an overwhelming dread of having to express himself in public. The young person raised in a verbally or physically abusive family may well show some evidence of trauma in later years.

Then there is another cause of fear that is often overlooked, but which for the purposes of this study may be more important than the temperamental, psychological, and environmental causes we have just considered. This cause is spiritual. To put it quite bluntly, sin can be the cause of great fears.

Uncertainty concerning the future is an overwhelming problem for countless people. That is no wonder when we consider the troubled environment in which we live!

On a global scale, there is marked uncertainty. World peace is as fragile as a porcelain figurine, and ideological forces of frightening power are flexing their muscles.

On a personal level, wives wonder if they are next in line to be traded in for a new model, as many of their friends have been. Children sit in their rooms alone with their stereos, worrying about whether their parents will stay together. Men are uncertain of their jobs, senior citizens are fearful of being able to afford the luxury of staying alive. Anxiety and indecision are often caused by the fear that comes from uncertainty about the future.

Guilt concerning the past is another great cause of fear. There is a skeleton hiding in the closet of most families, and the sheer fear of having the skeleton rattle its bones out in the open is enough to frighten many people out of their wits. This kind of fear is often demonstrated by worry, suspicion, and various withdrawal habits, coupled with depression. It is not uncommon for marriages to fall apart because one of the parties has been hiding the facts of premarital misbehavior from the other and lives in fear of the truth coming out. Businessmen who have evaded their taxes often have no chance to enjoy the money they "saved" because they spend all their time worrying that they are going to get caught by the IRS.

However, the biggest problem for most people lies neither in the past nor the future, but right now. Uncertainty concerning the future or guilt concerning the past are exceeded by inadequacy concerning the present.

You have seen nervous students break out in a rash before an examination. We are all familiar with business-men who have been intolerable at home when trying to finalize a big deal at work. Brides on their wedding day have been known to faint—as have bridegrooms! The sheer fear of not being able to cope is one of the most debilitating things known to humankind.

The big question is: can people who are afraid find some answers to their problems? The answer to that must, to a certain extent, be dependent on the specific causes of the fear. Those who have chronic problems in this area should seek professional help. But I am certain that many answers to fear can be found in Bible passages like the Psalms.

No Escape

There is much about spiritual living that raises the hack-les of unbelievers. One of the most infuriating things to them is what they call *escapism*. What I have just said about the Lord being the answer to many of our fears would fall into that category, in their thinking. But there is no thought of escape in David's mind. He's right where the action is hottest, and he intends to stay there; but while he's there, he is going to be confident as he trusts in the Lord.

This is the position of genuine believers who are in Christ. They are not looking for an escape from reality.

Drink and drugs do that. But Christians know Someone who allows them to face reality—however frightening it may be—Someone who enables them to live with reality and not to be overcome by it.

SHARE THE FAITH

"Wait for the LORD; be strong and take heart and wait for the LORD." (v. 14)

Time and space do not permit a fuller study of this psalm, but note the last verse: *"Wait for the LORD; be strong and take heart and wait for the LORD."* People who have learned to master fear can become an encourager of the fearful. They can recognize the symptoms of fear in friends and share their own experience of the Lord with them. This is great therapy as well as a great Christian principle. To know some answers and not share them is to do less than the Lord expects, while to minister to others the answer to life's fears is one of the quickest and safest routes to wholeness.

Psalm 32

1 Blessed is he
whose transgressions are forgiven
whose sins are covered.
2 Blessed is the man
whose sin the LORD does not count against him
and in whose spirit is no deceit.

3 When I kept silent,
my bones wasted away
through my groaning all the day long.
4 For day and night
your hand was heavy upon me;
my strength was sapped
as in the heat of summer. Selah.
5 Then I acknowledged my sin to you
and did not cover up my iniquity.
I said, "I will confess
my transgressions to the LORD"—
and you forgave
the guilt of my sin. Selah.

....

9 Do not be like the horse or the mule,
which have no understanding
but must be controlled by bit and bridle
or they will not come to you.
10 Many are the woes of the wicked,
but the LORD's unfailing love
surrounds the man who trusts in him.

CHAPTER EIGHT

WHEN YOU NEED
A LOT OF FORGIVENESS

When someone asked Martin Luther which were his favorite psalms, he said, "The Pauline psalms." His point was that, while Paul didn't write any psalms that we know of, he did quote David's psalms quite freely in his writings. Psalm 32 is one of those Paul quoted (see Romans 4:6–8). It is understandable that Luther enjoyed Paul's psalms so much because Luther had some real problems finding peace with God and a sense of forgiveness. He tried to do all that he had been taught but still felt guilty. When he finally understood from the Scriptures that salvation, forgiveness, justification, and all the other blessings of God are made available to us on the basis of God's grace rather than on our own efforts, he was almost beside himself with joy.

Paul was the great exponent of this doctrine of "justification by grace through faith," but he didn't invent it. David knew it. Abraham experienced it. In fact, down through the ages, men and women have come to God for the cleansing and forgiving they don't deserve but which God freely gives.

Like Paul and everyone else, David had his good days and his bad days. Sometimes he wrote psalms of somber quality, and other times he put an exuberant poem to music and sang to his heart's delight.

Psalm 32 is a song of joy. It starts with "Blessed is he" and finishes with "Rejoice in the LORD and be glad."

It is not hard to find the reason for David's joy. He has done something he ought not to have done, but, having accepted full responsibility for his actions and having repented fully of them, he knows he has been forgiven. There is nothing like forgiveness for making the heart sing and rejoice!

Augustine, the brilliant theologian of long ago, loved this psalm. This comes as no surprise to those who are aware of Augustine's reprobate life before his conversion to Christ. He, like David, had discovered the greatness of God's forgiveness and lived his life in the enjoyment of it.

When a young woman demonstrated her love and gratitude to the Lord in a rather overt fashion, the Pharisee in whose home the event took place expressed his disapproval. Jesus, however, said, "Her many sins have been forgiven—for she loved much. But he who has been forgiven little loves little" (Luke 7:47). Those who know what it is to be forgiven know what it is to love the Lord in an unashamed way. Forgiven much, they love much; and loving much, they show it in no uncertain terms. But there are many in the church who, like the Pharisee, are desperately embarrassed by any demonstration of love. Surely they would be much less inhibited in their love for the Lord if they were more overwhelmed with a sense of forgiveness.

FOUR KINDS OF SIN

"Blessed is he whose transgressions are forgiven, whose sins are covered. Blessed is the man whose sin the LORD does not count against him and in whose spirit is no deceit." (vv. 1–2)

The person on the street and the person on the pew often disagree. But they are strangely in accord in one unexpected area. The person on the street thinks that sin is killing and cheating and running around. The person on the pew thinks the same thing but quotes the Ten Commandments to prove it. The person on the pew also knows that the Bible condemns such things as pride, jealousy, greed, and lack of faith, but these things are not as important as the "big, bad sins." This error on the part of Christians is serious because sins like pride and jealousy and greed are the roots from which other sins spring. Roots are at least as important as fruits.

Because many people have failed to understand sin, they have little idea of the immensity of God's forgiveness. They think that they never did anything very bad, so God never had to forgive anything very big (which means that they probably won't love very greatly either). But what could be a greater sin than to deny God the right to be God? What could be more heinous than for puny humans to usurp the authority of almighty God? What could possibly be more objectionable to God than to have his creatures make the things he has given them more important than the one who gave them? Yet, there is not a person on this earth who has not been guilty of these sins on a continuing basis. These sins desperately need to be forgiven. These attitudes need to be rejected, for they have produced multitudes of sins before God.

The psalmist carefully spells out the variety and the enormity of our sins, in order that we might fully appreciate the far-reaching implications of God's incredible forgiveness. The psalm uses four words for sin: *transgression, sin, iniquity,* and *deceit*. Let's look at these more closely.

1. Transgression

To transgress is to trespass. When I was young, my parents and my brother and I used to take country walks on Sunday afternoons. One day I read a sign that said, "Trespassers will be prosecuted."

"Dad," I said, "what does that mean?"

"It means that if you go where you shouldn't, you'll be propped up and shot," he replied with a grin.

I heard the words, but I didn't understand the grin. Later, however, I learned that such notices let people know that there are places where they are not free to go, and that if they do, they must bear the consequences. This is the meaning of *transgression*.

God has outlined certain limits for human behavior and has made it quite clear that he expects human beings to operate within those limits—for their own good and for the well-being of society. But to a large extent the human race has transgressed these limits and has decided to cross them at will.

People may call this kind of behavior the "challenging of outdated social values" or the "overthrow of the repressive relics of the Victorian era." God has a shorter name for it: he calls it transgression. Every time you or I step over the God-given limits of human behavior, we transgress, and from that moment on, we are responsible for that sin. Try to figure out how many times you have stepped into the forbidden territory of jealousy or selfishness or independence. All of us need to be forgiven. Blessed is he or she whose transgressions are forgiven.

2. Sin

Liturgical services use a customary prayer of repentance that says, "We confess that we have sinned against you in thought, word, and deed, by what we have done, and by what we have left undone." Doing what we ought not to have done is to trespass or transgress; *not doing what we ought to have done* is *sin*.

There are numerous ways of knowing what we ought to do. Our conscience lets us know this quite regularly. The little voice inside whispers, "*Go on, speak out about that gross miscarriage of justice."* But the mind calculates, *If I do speak out, will it spoil my chances of promotion?* So silence reigns as sin is committed.

Horrific stories have appeared in the press concerning women being attacked in places where at least twenty-five people were within earshot. Bystanders heard but they didn't respond. *Don't get involved. Protect your own interests. You might get hurt.* So selfishness reigned as sin was perpetrated. God's commands to us are not always in the negative, "Thou shalt not." Many commands are negative, and they are the happy hunting grounds of trespassers. Many other commands are positive, "Thou shalt." They are the areas in which sin flourishes. Sit down and think about this. Try to evaluate the regularity with which you have failed to do what you ought to have done. All of those things need to be forgiven too.

3. Iniquity

Doing what we shouldn't and not doing what we should are the easiest areas of sinful behavior to understand. Now for something a little more complex. *Iniquity* (v. 2 KJV, NASB) is perverting what is right and making it into something wrong. It can sound great and yet be horrible. It can appear beautiful and yet be obnoxious.

For example, there are those who proclaim the gospel of peace in the political arena. They shout loud and long about the injustices under which people live. They promise great things in the name of freedom, but they don't always deliver. In fact, it is a sad thing to see what has been the lot of many who believed the evangelists of peace and freedom. They have found themselves in totalitarian regimes at best or in gulags at worst.

What about the "gift to charity" that is proclaimed as a sacrifice but is really nothing more than cheap advertising and a tax write-off? Or what do we say about the "prayer" offered in a small group that is nothing more than a tirade directed at another person present, with all the right people listening?

Peace is right. Freedom is right. Prayer and giving are right, but iniquity can get a stranglehold on them and make them wrong. Every time that happens, sin is committed and our weight of responsibility for that sin increases.

4. Deceit

Iniquity is the perverting of that which is right, but deceit is the projecting of that which is false. *Hypocrisy* is a good word to describe it, particularly when we remember that the root meaning of *hypocrisy* is "playacting," or "performing behind a mask." Unfortunately, for many of us we life our lives behind a mask.

A German friend of mine once ripped off my mask when I didn't even realize I was wearing one. He called me quite late one night and said, "Hello, how are you?"

I said, "Fine! Hey, it's good to hear your voice."

With great German candor he said, "Typical Englishman! Polite even when I wake you up at night. You are not pleased to hear my voice. You think I am stupid for calling at this hour. Why don't you say so?"

"All right, if you insist," I replied. "What on earth do you want at this hour of the night, you clown?"

But he was right. I was hiding behind my mask.

Things get much more serious, of course, when matters of greater importance are involved. In fact, we can get so caught up in our own deceit that we even play games with God. We tell him things we don't mean. We sing praises to him that aren't true. We make promises we have no intention of fulfilling. We become quite skilled at projecting that which is less than the truth.

Have you ever thought, *If only I had gotten into sin in a big way, I could have been forgiven in a big way, and then I couldn't help but love God in a big way?* Will you promise never to think like that again? Because the truth of the matter is, you *did* get into sin in a big way! Day after miserable day, you have transgressed and sinned and acted in iniquity and deceit. You have constantly done what was forbidden, have left undone what was required, have perverted that which is right, and have projected that which is false. But what a thrill to know that it is the greatness of your sin that qualifies you for the vastness of God's forgiveness. And it is the knowledge of God's forgiveness that leads to love and commitment.

THREE KINDS OF FORGIVENESS

"Blessed is he whose transgressions are forgiven, whose sins are covered. Blessed is the man whose sin the LORD does not count against him and in whose spirit is no deceit. (vv. 1–2)

There are three aspects of forgiveness that David mentions in this psalm. He uses the terms *forgiven, covered,* and *not counted against him.* Each of these terms has depths of meaning that we should understand.

1. Forgiven

We are all familiar with the term *scapegoat*. When a basketball team loses most of its games, something has to be done about it. The reason for the failure may well be that the team doesn't have any good players, but since they can't get rid of all the players, they have to find someone who can be held responsible. So they fire the coach. He becomes the scapegoat—the idea being that he is made responsible for the shortcomings of the whole outfit.

The original scapegoat was part of the Hebrew system of sacrifice and forgiveness. A goat would be selected by the high priest, who would lay his hands on its head; confess over it the sins, transgressions, and iniquities of all the people; and thereby, in ceremonial fashion, put the weight of the nation's sin on the goat. The animal was then sent away into the wilderness, and the children of Israel had a graphic reminder of how God puts our sins away from him. This is the basic meaning behind the word *forgiven* that David uses.

Since Christ came, the scapegoat is no longer necessary, for Christ himself bore our sins on the cross. He was separated from the Father because of our sins. He died and rose again, burying our sins "in the depths of the sea," removing them "as far as the east is from the west," so that God can now say to us, "I will remember your sins no more" (see Jeremiah 31:34; Hebrews 8:12). Many times I have prayed with people longing for forgiveness. They have testified to the inexpressible sense of relief that flooded their souls when they knew that their sins had been taken away.

2. Covered

"Blessed is he . . . whose sins are covered." God not only forgives our sins, he forgives them so thoroughly that he covers them completely—putting them out of his mind, out of remembrance, and out of sight. If we really grasp this great truth, our lives will be transformed.

Often I have found myself in a position where I have been required to forgive someone, but the thoughts that I harbor concerning that person reveal that my forgiving has certainly not included forgetting. But real forgiveness forgets.

During the time when I was writing this, I had to deal with a marital situation that was extremely serious because of the unfaithfulness of the wife. I believe there had been real confession and forgiveness, but the husband was going to have a struggle forgetting what had taken place. Eventually, I was sure he would, but for the present there would have to be a period of healing and reassuring in order for trust to be rebuilt. I think we can all understand this. But what a joy it is to know that God covers up our sins so effectively that they will never be thought of or discussed again.

My wife, Jill, told me that she was worried at one time about something she had done. As she was praying, she said, "Lord, you remember that awful thing I did." She sensed that he replied, "No, I don't remember. Jill, if you want to remember what I forgot, that's your privilege. But I would suggest you learn to forget what I have forgotten."

3. Not Counted

Not only does God forgive and forget our sins, he promises not to count our sins against us. He will not put our sins on our account. Obviously, all debts have to be charged to some account, and the great news of forgiveness is that God places our debts on Christ's account. He accepts full responsibility for them. That is the wonder of what Jesus did for us on Calvary.

The terrible debts that we could never repay have been transferred from our account, so we now have the possibility of living lives that will accumulate some real assets to the glory of God. When we begin to understand the greatness of our sin and the immeasurable depth of God's forgiveness, the foundation is laid for a whole new experience of life.

THE PAIN OF GUILT

"When I kept silent, my bones wasted away through my groaning all day long. For day and night your hand was heavy upon me; my strength was sapped as in the heat of summer." (vv. 3–4)

And yet the experience of finding forgiveness is not without its pressures. David explains something of the battle that went on in his life as he became increasingly conscious of his sin and more aware of the necessity of dealing with it. David was under considerable pressure from the Lord, which he describes in such graphic phrases as, *"my bones wasted away through my groaning . . . your hand was heavy upon me . . . my strength was sapped as in the heat of summer."*

In other words, David was suffering from such guilt and conviction that he was dry and depressed and thoroughly upset. The longer he *"kept silent"* about his sin, the worse it became, but when he came to the point of acknowledging and confessing, he was able to say, "You forgave the guilt of my sin" (v. 5).

BITS AND BRIDLES

"Do not be like the horse or the mule, which have no understanding but must be controlled by bit and bridle or they will not come to you." (v. 9)

Beware of the mistaken idea that once confession has been made and forgiveness has been received, we as Christians are free to go on with our lives as before. Be clear in your mind that being forgiven does not leave you free to go on in the same way. Rather, it introduces you to a new responsibility to be different. When the Lord forgave the woman who had committed adultery, he didn't say, "Okay, forget it." He insisted that, having been forgiven, she should, "Go now and leave your life of sin" (John 8:11). David likewise counsels us not to be like an unthinking horse that has to be held by bit and bridle to keep him under control, but to open ourselves up to the instructions of the Lord and to act in obedience to him. When we submit to God's instruction, he will guide us. And he will not lead us into temptation but will deliver us from evil. Our experience of forgiveness will grow ever deeper as we depend on the Lord to instruct and respond in obedience to his instruction. When we do this, we can be sure that he will lead us in the right path.

LOVE WILL SURROUND US

"Many are the woes of the wicked, but the LORD's unfailing love surrounds the man who trusts in him." (v. 10)

Being surrounded by hostility makes people edgy and suspicious. What happens, then, to people who are surrounded by God's love? They begin to respond in more loving ways to others. The forgiven are great forgivers. From the moment they receive God's mercy, they desire to freely forgive.

Some years ago a young woman came to my study, very distressed. She had made a commitment to the Lord a few days earlier but had asked to see me because something was troubling her. She poured out a long story concerning an affair she had been having with one of her husband's friends. Then she insisted that her husband should know and that I should tell him! That was a new experience for me.

After some discussion with the woman, I called the husband. When he arrived at my study, I told him what had happened. His response was a remarkable and beautiful thing to behold. Turning to his tearful and fearful wife, he said, "I love you. I forgive you. Let's make a new start."

Many things had to be straightened out, and much hurt had to be healed, but his response of forgiveness, made possible by his own understanding of the forgiveness of God, became the basis of a new joy and a new life.

Bitterness and harshness do not belong in the forgiven heart. Love and joy and forgiveness should flourish there. In your experience of the forgiveness of God, learn to forgive the boss who abused your willing spirit, the church that failed to meet your expectations, the spouse who hurt you, and the prodigal children who disgraced you. God forgave you, didn't he? Shouldn't you do the same?

Psalm 37

1 Do not fret because of evil men
or be envious of those who do wrong;
2 for like the grass they will soon wither,
like green plants they will soon die away.

3 Trust in the LORD and do good;
dwell in the land and enjoy safe pasture.
4 Delight yourself in the LORD
and he will give you the desires of your heart.

5 Commit your way to the LORD;
trust in him and he will do this:
6 He will make your righteousness shine like the dawn,
the justice of your cause like the noonday sun.

7 Be still before the LORD and wait patiently for him;
do not fret when men succeed in their ways,
when they carry out their wicked schemes.

8 Refrain from anger and turn from wrath;
do not fret—it leads only to evil.
9 For evil men will be cut off,
but those who hope in the LORD will inherit the land.

10 A little while, and the wicked will be no more;
though you look for them, they will not be found.
11 But the meek will inherit the land and enjoy great peace.

....

13 but the Lord laughs at the wicked,
for he knows their day is coming.

14 The wicked draw the sword
and bend the bow
to bring down the poor and needy,
to slay those whose ways are upright.

....

17 for the power of the wicked will be broken,
   but the LORD upholds the righteous.

18 The days of the blameless are known to the LORD,
   and their inheritance will endure forever.
19 In times of disaster they will not wither;
   in days of famine they will enjoy plenty.

20 But the wicked will perish:
The LORD's enemies will be like the beauty of the fields,
   they will vanish—vanish like smoke.

21 The wicked borrow and do not repay,
   but the righteous give generously;

....

23 If the LORD delights in a man's way,
   he makes his steps firm;
24 though he stumble, he will not fall,
   for the Lord upholds him with his hand.
25 I was young and now I am old,
yet I have never seen the righteous forsaken
   or their children begging bread.

....

27 Turn from evil and do good;
   then you will dwell in the land forever.
28 For the LORD loves the just
   and will not forsake his faithful ones.

CHAPTER NINE

WHEN BEING GOOD
DOESN'T SEEM TO PAY

Few things are more infuriating than seeing criminals go free while honest people suffer. There is nothing more disturbing than knowing that the hard-hit will get hit harder while the protected will get more protection. This is particularly true if you are trying to do the right thing and it goes sour on you, while people around you are not even trying to do right and life is sweet for them.

The unfairness and injustice of life is one of the hardest things for many people to take! We may even get so envious of the people who go their merry way of irresponsibility and illegitimacy that we feel our struggle for righteousness and justice is all in vain.

Others seem to get away with murder, and you can't get away with anything. You try to do an honest day's work. You endeavor to be honest and thrifty. But the more you try to do things right, the more you find you are not appreciated. You may even be ridiculed, while other people get all the praise.

When you look at some of the people in high places,

you know they got there by shady means and stay there by even shadier tactics, and nothing can be done about it.

You know your boss is "adjusting" his tax returns, but he gets away with it. He has a plush office and an administrative assistant, while your office is so small you have to go outside to turn a page. And you answer your own phone.

You know a kid who got busted for drugs when he was innocent. He was framed by an unscrupulous cop. The kid is in jail and the cop is free. It's all very maddening.

If this sounds unspiritual, tell David, because these were the kinds of thoughts that passed through his mind at times. Such thoughts should be in the mind of spiritual people because they should recognize the injustices in the world caused by people's refusal to obey God's principles. Spiritually minded people must not close their eyes to these things. They should inquire and search and deal with these issues. In Psalm 37 David reveals that he had been fully acquainted with evil people, those who do wrong and who "carry out their wicked schemes" and yet who succeed.

TRUST AND DO
"Trust in the LORD and do good...." (v. 3a)

This psalm contains some very specific instructions for those who endure injustice and who understand that God will finally triumph and good will ultimately prevail. I am glad for these instructions because simply believing that "it will all come out in the wash" and that "there'll be a brighter day tomorrow" leaves something to be desired in terms of knowing exactly how to cope now.

"Trust in the LORD and do good" is easy enough to understand, if not always easy to do. This heart attitude of trust in the Lord, who will ultimately triumph and who is committed to rewarding right and punishing wrong, is vital. If I can trust God to work out the final results, I need not worry about them myself. This leaves me free to get on with doing the right thing, knowing that God will deal with the guy who is doing the wrong thing. My natural tendency is to do just the opposite. I feel inclined to go after the guy who did the wrong thing and make him pay for it, while ignoring the very thing that God has told me to do.

Apply this, for example, to marriage. A husband does something wrong and harms the relationship. The wife finds out and devotes all her energy and considerable talents thereafter to make him pay for it. She withdraws from all expressions of intimacy and generally concentrates on getting even. Rejection and vengeance don't help anything; they only make matters a thousand times worse. No doubt she had a raw deal. No one disputes that. But there is equally no doubt that she reacted to injustice the wrong way. She should have said to her husband, "What you did was wrong, and you're answerable to God, so I'll let him deal with you. Since I'm answerable to him too, I'm going to concentrate on doing the right thing by you." That is trusting God to do his part and obeying God by doing your part. Trusting and doing.

DELIGHT AND DESIRE

"Delight yourself in the LORD and he will give you the desires of your heart." (v. 4)

An unfortunate thing about injustice is that it makes you concentrate on it. When something goes wrong, it is sometimes difficult to remember all the things that have gone right. When wrongs are committed against us, we seem to remember them with amazing accuracy. Amid injustice, it's often difficult to remember the Lord. But David insisted that we should delight ourselves in God. To delight in the Lord while suffering injustice requires great discipline of mind and will. But there is a beautiful incentive: *"he will give you the desires of your heart."* This promise needs a little explanation because it can easily be misunderstood. It does not mean that you can ask for and anticipate receiving anything your selfish heart may desire. It means that if the Lord is your sole delight, he will give you desires that are new and beautiful. Your desires will originate with the Lord.

Think about all the possibilities! If the wife we described were to delight in the Lord instead of riveting her attention on her raw deal, she would get a whole new set of desires from him. She would desire to work out a reconciliation instead of concentrating on revenge. She would desire to show grace more than grief, and love more than hate. And that transformation would certainly be to everyone's advantage.

COMMIT AND TRUST

"Commit your way to the LORD; trust in him and he will do this: He will make your righteousness shine like the dawn, the justice of your cause like the noonday sun."
(vv. 5–6)

Once injustice has been experienced, reaction sets in immediately. If this is not dealt with quickly, the shoulder may develop a chip. Chips soon become personal crusades, and in no time at all injustice will be added to injustice.

There is another approach to the problem. The Lord Jesus used it to great effect. "When they hurled their insults at him, he did not retaliate; . . . Instead, he entrusted himself to him who judges justly" (1 Peter 2:23). This approach did not allow Christ to escape the cross, but it did allow him to glorify the Father in the way he handled personal injustice. And how did he handle it? By committing himself to the righteous Judge who will one day balance the scales of justice once and for all.

This is exactly what the psalmist insists *we* should do. But notice that in addition to committing our way to the Lord he says, *"trust in him."*

Some years ago I was preaching in a town, and a woman had accepted responsibility for getting me to the church on time. She had a large car, which she filled with a large number of friends. I had to squeeze into a tiny space in the backseat. We took off down the road at a terrifying pace and shot straight through a stop sign. Quite frankly, I was frightened out of my evangelical mind.

The main problem was that the lady insisted on talking face to face with me at the same time she was driving. Since I was huddled in the backseat, you can understand that this meant that she couldn't concentrate on both me and the road. She chose me.

By stepping into her car, I had committed myself to her driving, but I can assure you that after the first few yards I didn't trust her at all. You will find that a commitment made to Christ may similarly wear thin when unwanted things happen. But David exhorts us to *"trust in him."* And the result of this trusting and committing will be that *"he will make your righteousness shine like the dawn, the justice of your cause like the noonday sun."* It is just as if the Lord were saying, "Don't try to deal with the injustices of life yourself. Trust me and I will handle your case."

REST AND WAIT

*"Be still before the LORD and
wait patiently for him. . . ."* (v. 7a)

No doubt some of you are ready to retort, "That's okay, but how do you expect me to sit back and take all this abuse without any kind of reaction?" I agree that would not be a natural response, but that is what makes it so interesting. It is a spiritual response. Instead of handling the thing yourself, you learn to trust God to work on your own injustices, and you are content to believe that God will ultimately work things out.

That word ultimately adds a dimension that is so often missing. We tend to want immediate answers to our problems and immediate correction of our ills. But God does not work at our frantic pace. He sees things in the light of eternity rather than in the glare of time. God is thinking of perfecting people for glory rather than protecting people from temporary unpleasantness. In fact, he may use the injustice and the unpleasantness as a lesson to lead us further in our relationship with him. The apostle Paul certainly learned things in prison that he would never have learned elsewhere. I'm sure that he often thought his treatment was unjust. Nevertheless, he learned to be patient and faithful in his smelly cell. Like David, his attitude was to "be still before the LORD and wait patiently for him."

THREE DON'TS

"Refrain from anger and turn from wrath; do not fret—
it leads only to evil." (v. 8)

First, don't get mad about it. "Refrain from anger." Plenty of people in plenty of places are getting plenty mad about what has happened to them. And I can understand their being upset. But the Lord has told us that if we really trust him in our lives, it is not necessary or helpful for us to get angry about the injustices we suffer.

Second, "turn from wrath." Wrath goes a step further than anger. It is a vicious fury marked by a desire for vengeance. But Romans 12:19 tells us to leave vengeance to the Lord. Our path is to be one of peace. Anger and wrath are no cure for injustice.

Third, *"do not fret."* The word *fret* means literally "to burn or consume." So we can say "don't get hot under the collar" about what is happening to you. Don't let it eat you up day after day. Don't get so consumed with it that you are unable to think of anything else. Don't focus on fret.

GOOD WILL EVENTUALLY PREVAIL

"For evil men will be cut off, but those who hope in the LORD will inherit the land. A little while, and the wicked will be no more; though you look for them, they will not be found. But the meek will inherit the land and enjoy great peace. . . . The Lord laughs at the wicked, for he knows their day is coming." (vv. 9–11, 13)

It is a short step from the triumph of God to the prevailing of good. God and good are closely related. Read the verses above carefully, and examine all the statements concerning the eventual destruction of wickedness and the wicked one. Then, in total contrast, check the statements regarding those who have faithfully followed the Lord.

The wicked are going to see their plans backfire on them, their riches dissipate, and their empires crumble. It is not too difficult to understand this even from a study of modern history. The wicked prosper, the unscrupulous strut around, the rogues laugh, and the rascals grin and wink—but where are their predecessors? It is not necessary to name names, but those who used to hold power unjustly have fallen and departed. They have gone to their reward, and the gains of their abuses have gone into other pockets.

Empires built on injustice have fallen! Power structures based on avarice have left the greedy both empty-handed and empty-hearted. This is how it has always been, and this is how it is going to be till the end of time.

Meanwhile, those who endeavor to resist the pressures and swim against the tide will finally discover that they chose the right course. In words reminiscent of the Sermon on the Mount, David says, *"The meek will inherit the land and enjoy great peace."*

THE DIFFICULT ROAD

"The wicked draw the sword and bend the bow to bring down the poor and needy, to slay those whose ways are upright. . . . The wicked borrow and do not repay, but the righteous give generously. . . ." (vv. 14, 21)

People who try to do things God's way have a difficult road ahead of them. They are called to a life of conflict. Given a choice between a life of comfort and a life of conflict, most people naturally choose the former. But the one who is committed to Christ has, in making that commitment, chosen the latter. To go Christ's way means exactly going his way—and he went the way of the cross.

Christ suffered not only the agony of Calvary's cross but

the anguish of rejection and the pain of misrepresentation. He knew what David meant when he talked of the wicked working *"to slay those whose ways are upright."* This adds further pressure to the believer because, having chosen to follow Christ in the path of conflict, he or she often is attacked by those who are committed to nothing at all.

Turning the other cheek gets wearisome after a while. Giving rather than receiving becomes expensive. Especially when you have the obligation to give, but the receiver feels no responsibility to return anything. *"The wicked borrow and do not repay, but the righteous give generously."*

Having your good works abused, your sincere desire to help ridiculed, your sacrificial living mocked, and your responsible lifestyle turned to the advantage of the unscrupulous is hard to take. But such conflict and sacrifice and discipline are the ingredients that, mixed with faith, make a vital spiritual experience.

GOD WILL ULTIMATELY TRIUMPH

"For the power of the wicked will be broken, but the LORD upholds the righteous. The days of the blameless are known to the LORD, and their inheritance will endure forever. The LORD's enemies . . . will vanish. . . ." (vv. 17–18, 20)

Living in a world full of meaningless injustice and exploitation can wear on us. Feeling that everything is hopeless and useless, we may want to give up. But taking this course is not acceptable because it discounts the Lord. Through all our turmoil and disaster shines the fact that

God has gone on record assuring us that he will ultimately triumph. We have seen this repeatedly in the psalms, but specific phrases illustrate it in Psalm 37. *"The LORD upholds the righteous"*; *"the days of the blameless are known to the LORD"*; *"the LORD's enemies . . . will vanish."*

Through all the difficulties of spiritual experience, the Lord will bring his people to an inheritance that *"will endure forever."* This is a blow to all the forces that oppose the saints, for these forces can't win. They can frustrate and infuriate and intimidate, but they can't obliterate, because the Lord has reserved the final triumph for himself. All the agencies of oppression that have unjustly worked in disregard of God's principles will finally be thwarted. One day they will have to watch those they despised and oppressed rejoicing in glory.

Those same hostile forces will also feel the triumph of God in their own experience. "The wicked will perish" (v. 20). The Lord has stated categorically that everyone who practices injustice, who specializes in oppression, who scorns divine principle had better beware: "Their day is coming" (v. 13).

DOWN BUT NOT OUT!

"If the LORD delights in a man's way, he makes his steps firm; though he stumble, he will not fall, for the LORD upholds him with his hand." (vv. 23–24)

Furthermore, the good person steps out, knowing that the Lord has made *"his steps firm."* Of course, some of those steps are steep, and many a well-meaning believer has tripped over the most trifling problem, but even when this happens, he has the assurance that *"though he stumble, he will not fall,"* or, in the words of the King James Version, "though he fall, he shall not be utterly cast down." Down he may be, but not out!

When we firmly grasp and truly believe these principles, then we can trust God in all our circumstances and learn to cope with the injustice and abuse we see around us. And what's more, we will demonstrate to a watching world the reserves of strength and resources for living that many of them do not possess. In this way, we will have a testimony to the world that is sadly needed today.

The early church clearly showed to an incredulous world that Christians could endure unbelievable abuse, suffer incredible hardship, and yet triumph so thoroughly that even their oppressors and abusers were compelled to come to Christ. The same has been the case in many churches under totalitarian regimes and in areas of the world where suffering has become a way of life.

THE WISDOM OF EXPERIENCE
"I was young and now I am old. . . ." (v. 25)

Hotheads lose control; cool heads prevail. Inexperience overreacts; experience calculates more carefully. David wrote this psalm from the vantage point of old age. He had come a long way from the sheepfold of his youth. It was no fresh-faced shepherd boy talking here, but a veteran herdsman who could say, *"I was young and now I am old."* Years of hard experience had mellowed David into a man of deep insight, integrity, and balance. Innumerable experiences of failure and success, disappointment and delight had left their marks on him. But his conviction concerning his Lord, his faith in him, and his absolute assurance that he would ultimately reign in righteousness had never wavered. David proclaimed this loud and clear.

WHAT ABOUT SOCIAL INJUSTICE?

"Turn from evil and do good; then you will dwell in the land forever. For the LORD loves the just and will not forsake his faithful ones." (vv. 27–28)

When the Scripture speaks against reacting to personal injustice, it is not referring to the reactions we should have to the social injustices being dished out to others. It is my firm conviction that those who love the Lord and respect his ways should be constantly on the alert for abuses of his principles in society. They should be ready, in the Lord's name, to act on behalf of the oppressed. But in all their activities, they should never stoop to evil. We cannot do evil in hope that good may come of it

Psalm 42

¹ As the deer pants for streams of water,
so my soul pants for you, O God.
² My soul thirsts for God, for the living God.
When can I go and meet with God?
³ My tears have been my food
day and night,
while men say to me all day long,
"Where is your God?"
⁴ These things I remember
as I pour out my soul:
how I used to go with the multitude,
leading the procession to the house of God,
with shouts of joy and thanksgiving
among the festive throng.

⁵ Why are you downcast, O my soul?
Why so disturbed within me?
Put your hope in God,
for I will yet praise him,
my Savior and ⁶ my God.

My soul is downcast within me;
therefore I will remember you
from the land of the Jordan,
the heights of Hermon—from Mount Mizar.
⁷ Deep calls to deep
in the roar of your waterfalls,
all your waves and breakers
have swept over me.

⁸ By day the LORD directs his love,
at night his song is with me—
a prayer to the God of my life.

⁹ I say to God my Rock,

"Why have you forgotten me?
Why must I go about mourning,
Oppressed by the enemy?"
10 *My bones suffer mortal agony*
as my foes taunt me,
saying to me all day long,
"Where is your God?"

11 *Why are you downcast, O my soul?*
Why so disturbed within me?
Put your hope in God,
for I will yet praise him,
my Savior and my God.

CHAPTER TEN

WHEN DEPRESSION BLANKETS YOU
LIKE A CLOUD

Depression is all too common in today's world. The offices of doctors and psychiatrists, pastors and counselors are full to overflowing with people suffering from this condition. And it's nothing new.

Winston Churchill, one of the great leaders of human history, suffered terribly from depression. He said it followed him like "a black dog."

Ernest Hemingway, the rugged author of bestsellers like *For Whom the Bell Tolls* and *The Old Man and the Sea*, had such a problem in this area that he eventually took his own life.

Abraham Lincoln, whose "House Divided against Itself" speech helped to win him the presidency, knew awful, divisive doubt and depression in his own life.

Charles Haddon Spurgeon, one of the greatest preachers of all time, who was known for his sparkling wit and quick humor, nevertheless had a lifetime battle with depression that was caused by gout, the disease that led to his death at the age of fifty-eight.

Most of us are familiar with the despondent look of those who are depressed. Everywhere we see people who

are sinking under their heavy circumstances. Tears and sighs, tales of woe and stories of broken hearts abound. Many depressed people live alone. Their main source of company is the television, which makes them even more depressed. Soap operas churn out hours of coffee-cup discourses almost exclusively devoted to the nonresolution of problems. Satellite dishes and cable companies bring hundreds of channels with news about the depressing truth of our contemporary world right into their living rooms. Dramatic presentations seem to have a chilling infatuation with the more depressing aspects of our society. About the only relief available comes from the comedy programs, and they don't solve anything. They just help escape reality for a half hour or so.

Depression is a major problem that affects more people than we imagine and infects them more than we realize.

WHAT CAUSES DEPRESSION?

No doubt some people, because of their temperaments, are more prone to depression than others. If they tend to be introspective, there is more chance of their getting depressed than if they are extroverts.

But while introverts are more prone to depression than others, they are also usually more sensitive and concerned than others. So being an introvert is not all bad! Dr. Martyn Lloyd-Jones in his book *Spiritual Depression* writes, "Indeed, I could make out a good case for saying that quite often the people who stand out most gloriously in the history of the church are people of the very type we are now considering. Some of the greatest saints belong to the introverts."

Physical disability or chemical imbalances in the body can also lead to depression. In Spurgeon's case this was certainly true. Gout is an extremely painful illness centering in the big toe, of all places. (I'm sure even Spurgeon's humor had a hard time seeing the funny side of that at times!) But you don't have to suffer from gout to be depressed. Being overtired, under undue stress for a sustained period, or having a prolonged illness will eventually cause some form of depression.

SPIRITUAL DEPRESSION

I do not want to fall into the error of separating spiritual depression from depression caused by temperament or physical disability. People are spirit, soul, and body, and all three are intricately bound up together. But some people are depressed primarily because they have some real problems of the spirit. Sin can get one terribly down. Guilt can become so pervasive that it can immobilize a person. And we must not forget the considerable power of Satan as he works in people's lives and leads them into the valley of depression.

One day as I was packing to go on a preaching trip to the Orient, I received an urgent call to someone's home. Arriving there, I found the man of the house sitting still, looking at a point on the wall. His wife said he had been in that position for hours.

I told him, "You need to see a doctor because you may

have a physical problem. He may recommend a psychologist if he thinks you have an emotional problem. But if you have a spiritual problem, I may be able to help."

As soon as I said "spiritual," he showed the first sign of interest. So I explained forgiveness, justification, hope, heaven, eternal life, and all kinds of things that the Lord offers in the bundle of salvation. Suddenly, he said, "I want to be forgiven." At that point I got cold feet. What if he had a tumor? I would be making matters worse. I felt strangely in over my head but, asking the Lord for wisdom, I took a deep breath and led the man in prayer.

DAVID'S DEPRESSION

"As the deer pants for streams of water, so my soul pants for you, O God. . . . When can I go and meet with God? My tears have been my food day and night, while men say to me all day long, 'Where is your God?' These things I remember as I pour out my soul: how I used to go with the multitude, leading the procession to the house of God, with shouts of joy and thanksgiving among the festive throng." (vv. 1–4)

The great people of the Bible were not immune to depression. John the Baptist understandably got depressed when he lay in his cell wondering what the Messiah was doing. Jeremiah wept copiously over the destruction of Jerusalem and because his own circumstances went from bad to worse. Job scratched his diseased flesh with a broken piece of pottery as he listened to his depressing friends give their advice. Elijah fell into a dark hole of depression after his victory on Mount Carmel.

But David's experience of depression as recorded in Psalm 42 is particularly helpful because he has much to say about how it felt and what he did about it. I often recommend a careful reading of this psalm to those who are having troubles with depression.

The circumstances of David's life were such that he had been deprived of many things he held dear. Not the least was his regular attendance at a place of worship. It may seem to us that he was too dependent on the place and that he should have been able to worship the Lord anywhere. In all fairness, though, we have to admit that places and people play a big part in our experience of the Lord. So great was David's disappointment that he felt he had lost the sense of God's presence. There was a tinge of desperation in his voice when he said, "As the deer pants for streams of water, so my soul pants for you, O God" (v. 1).

The Sneers of Others

People hadn't helped David much either. Some of them had taken the opportunity to kick him while he was down. Continually they had been sneering at him, "Where is your God?" This only served to upset David more. It's bad enough being out of touch with the Lord, but it is ten times worse when people notice it and start to deride you because of it.

Self-Pity

David's tears had flowed, but I want you to note that he said, *"My tears have been my food day and night."* He had fallen into the state of feeling so sorry for himself that he was feeding on his unfortunate situation. This led him deeper into depression. There was no relief. Day and night he cried. Hour after hour he succumbed to his feelings. There appeared to be no way out of his predicament.

David's mind was fixed on his sorrows: *"These things I remember."* Over and over he dwelt on the dismal disappointments of his life until he could think of nothing else. He shared these things with nobody. Brooding alone he said, *"I pour out my soul."* Living in the fading memories of the "good old days," he recounted, *"How I used to go with the multitude, leading the procession to the house of God, with shouts of joy and thanksgiving."*

The details of David's circumstances may differ from ours, but the experience of his depression is not at all removed from the symptoms suffered by so many. Self-pity, brooding, withdrawal, morose reminiscing, and introspection have been the painful lot of the depressed in all ages.

8 SPIRITUAL STEPS FOR OVERCOMING DEPRESSION

Fortunately David did not only recount his depression. He went into some detail as to how he coped with his feelings.

1. Admit the Truth

"Why are you downcast, O my soul?" (v. 5a)

The first thing to note is that David was realistic enough to admit that he was depressed. *"Why are you downcast, O my soul?"* he asked. There was no evasion on his part. He was depressed and he knew it well, and he was rapidly prepared to admit it.

Not everyone who is depressed is prepared to be realistic in this way. It is sometimes easier to dwell on the unfortunate circumstances in which you find yourself than to admit that you are in bad shape. It's your inward condition, not your outward circumstances, that is really important.

If a person gets shot in the leg, there are two courses she could follow. She could sit down and ponder the fact that she got shot, take a photograph of her wound, study books on ballistics, and take a course on the psychological aberrations of potential assassins. Or she could say, "I'm shot. Get me to the doctor!"

If you've never done it before, do it now. Say aloud, "I am depressed!"

2. Try a Little Detective Work

"Why [is my soul] so disturbed within me?" (v. 5b)

Once you have been honest about your condition, it is time for a little detective work. Start delving into the situation in which you find yourself. Ask some pertinent questions. If you can't think of any helpful questions, find a trusted friend who will level with you about how he or she sees your situation. Then start asking yourself, "Why is my soul so disturbed? Why, why, why?"

But be very careful. David is not getting further into his self-pity, asking, "Why did this have to happen to me?" or "Why can't someone else have some bad luck instead of it always being me?" His question is factual and pertinent. "Why are you depressed, my soul?"

This question, if handled honestly, may lead a depressed person into some deep personal discoveries. For instance, she may discover that her depression is the result of resentment. Because of disappointment with life, she may have become angry with God and everyone else, and sunk lower and lower into a resentful mire.

Another depressed person may discover that subconsciously he had come to feel that he had a divine right of immunity from all problems. He may never have come to the elementary understanding that problems are inevitable in a sin-distorted world, that no one goes through life smelling only roses.

Depressed people make discoveries like this only when they are wise enough to investigate into their own lives. Then they have to adjust to the answers they find. It is relatively simple to wallow in self-pity if you feel that the world did you wrong and you always did it right. But it's

not at all easy to confront the fact that your depression is
the result of childish resentment or superficial thinking.

3. Report Back to Yourself

"Put your hope in God. . . ." (v. 5c)

All good detectives make reports and so should you.
Having made inquiries about the causes of your depression and having learned some of those causes, you should
then "make an appointment with yourself" and present
the facts to yourself. Notice that there is a major difference
between allowing your depressed state to talk to you, and
you confronting and talking to your depressed state. If this
sounds a little like "gobbledygook," believe me, it isn't.

Do what King David did. Give your soul a good talking to! "Listen to me, soul. I've listened to your whining
and moaning long enough. I've had enough of this
because it is not solving anything. You have been
'downcast' long enough. You have been 'disturbed
within me' far too long. It's time for something different
in my life." Before you decide that this approach is nothing more than mind over matter, let me tell you what
else David said to his soul: *"Put your hope in God."* Now,
that's an order!

I have known some people who couldn't drag themselves out of depression if their lives depended on it. But I
have known many more who could, if they would only
tell themselves to "put your hope in God." When people

162

start looking at the Lord and his attributes and abilities instead of focusing on their own failings and situations, I believe they turn the corner toward emotional peace. But make no mistake, a definite act of the will is required!

4. Determine to Remember God

". . . for I will yet praise him, my Savior and my God. . . . I will remember you . . ." (vv. 5d–e; 6b)

When it came to dealing with his depression, note what David said, *"I will yet praise him."* He was saying, "I *will* remember God. I *will* speak to him. I *will* thank him." Everybody has a will (though some people seem to have more of a "won't"), and this will has to be put into gear if depression is to be handled adequately.

I am aware, course, that in extreme cases of depression, people can lose the will to will. Before they can take the spiritual steps that we are concentrating on in this discussion of an ancient psalm, they may often need the ministry and help of a godly trained counselor or even require specialized medical care.

Yet David determined, with his will, to remember the Lord, even though the very environment in which he found himself was hostile. He only had to look around to be reminded of the circumstances that depressed him, but he made up his mind to look away from his immediate surroundings to the Lord. He had to concentrate on the Lord to succeed, but he believed God would enable him to do so.

You must learn to do this. If it is your hospital room that depresses you, make a definite decision to turn your eyes from the bed to the Bible. If it is your small children who are getting you down, turn your eyes from the diapers once in a while to the crown that will be yours when you have brought up your children to the glory of God.

Another thing: don't keep the depression bottled up inside. Make up your mind to say to God what is on your heart. Say it aloud. Not because he is hard of hearing, but because it is good for you to listen to what you expect *him* to listen to! Start talking to him. Make up your mind to do this. It will stop your pouting and start you moving.

The word *praise* may seem strangely out of place in a discussion of depression, but it appears in the psalm on depression, so it must be fitting. *"I will yet praise him,"* said David. To understand this you must take a look at the things David said about the Lord, and the special relationship David and the Lord enjoyed together. David's heart became so full of considerations of his God that he found his lips and heart breaking out in overflowing praise and thanksgiving.

I know of no better cure for depression than praise. Not the empty noise that some people seem to mistake for praise. Nor do we need the evasion of truth and the escape into unreality that some people call victory. But the intelligent concentration of the mind on the Lord, to such a degree that the heart becomes warm from the truth the mind is pondering, can work wonders.

5. Meditate—Don't Mope

"God of my life . . . God my Rock . . ." (vv. 8c–9a)

Meditation has become increasingly popular in our culture through the influence of Eastern religions. In our frantic Western world, it is not difficult to understand why a lot of exhausted people have gone for meditation like salmon go for flies. There is dangerous nonsense inherent in much of this philosophy. However, this does not diminish the need for meditation.

The meditation of which Scripture speaks bears little resemblance to the mystical activities of the assorted Eastern gurus who have come our way. They prescribe monosyllabic mantras, like "Om," on which the devotee must meditate. David had a lot more than "Om" in mind! When David meditated, he thought about the Lord in numerous, specific ways. Moping was no longer the order of the day. His God became the focal point of his attention.

Notice carefully the details of David's thoughts, once his thinking got around to the Lord. First, he thought about the *"God of my life."* It is one thing to believe in God, but not know where or what he is. It is quite a different matter to believe that the one true and living God is the *"God of my life."* This is a thrilling concept, for it embraces every part of a person's being. Even the part called depression.

If God is the God of my life, presumably he is God enough to be God in the things that depress me! A broken leg may depress you if you don't believe in a God who is bigger than a broken leg. A business setback may plunge you into the depths for a month or so, unless God is so much the God of your life that he is in reality the God of your business.

Then David talked about God as his "*Rock*." No longer filled with the poison of self-pity and fixation on the morbid, David is filled with thoughts of a Lord who is unsinkable and whose goodness is unmeasurable. Now, that's the sort of thing a depressed person should meditate on! When all seems lost, and you have an awful sinking feeling, what could be better than to know that there is a rock beneath you upon which you can stand when you're through sinking! God your Rock can bear your weight. He will not shift his position.

6. Bring the Lord into the Depression

"Why have you forgotten me?" (v. 9b)

David took one more vital step: he related his depression to the Lord. It is no accident that the Lord is mentioned or referred to at least once in every verse of this psalm—not always in the right way, but at least he is mentioned!

"Why have you forgotten me?" is a very honest question. David felt that the Lord had overlooked his plight. And it is easy for us to feel the same way. You don't need too many awkward situations before you are tempted to

question God's relevance, his faithfulness, or even his very existence.

A little elementary Bible knowledge at this point goes a long way. "Never will I leave you; never will I forsake you" (Hebrews 13:5) and "Surely I am with you always" (Matthew 28:20) are straightforward promises from the God who cannot lie. Provided we keep what we believe in front of how we feel, we can cope with temptations to doubt God. But if we allow how we feel to alter what we believe, we are in deep trouble.

A man may wake up feeling not very married. He goes to work and sees a pretty woman in the office and in no time at all he behaves as if he were not married. This would never have happened if he had kept that fact of his marital *commitment* in the forefront of his mind, instead of allowing his *feelings* about his marriage to dominate. So it is with our relationship with the Lord.

7. Turn to God for Health

> "... [He] is the health of my countenance, and my God."
> (v. 11e KJV)

In the newer Bible translations, verse 11 (which is almost identical to verse 5) says, "my Savior and my God." The King James Version renders this verse *"the health of my countenance, and my God."* This is a beautiful expression. Depressed people often show on their faces what is going on inside their heads. But the Lord can make all the difference. He can bring hope and health to a fallen countenance. He can so fill your thoughts that you get your mind off yourself and your woes and onto him and his abundant blessings. When this happens, your face will look different.

8. Hope in God

"Put your hope in God. . . ." (v. 11c)

One more thing remains to be said: after careful self-evaluation, self-confrontation, and self-discipline comes the direct command to the depressed soul: *"Put your hope in God."* This is crucial. It is the final key to overcoming depression.

FINDING YOUR WAY BACK

When a believer sinks into a spiritual depression, it is because of lost hope, lost confidence, lost trust. Next time that happens to you, work through the eight spiritual steps outlined in this chapter, focusing on the final and most crucial step: *"Put your hope in God."*

So don't despair if you struggle with depression. As best you can, put your trust where it belongs, and God will put your depression where it belongs—in the depths of the sea.

Psalm 46

1 *God is our refuge and strength*
an ever-present help in trouble.
2 *Therefore we will not fear, though the earth give way*
and the mountains fall into the heart of the sea,
3 *though its waters roar and foam*
and the mountains quake with their surging. Selah

4 *There is a river whose streams make glad the city of God,*
the holy place where the Most High dwells.
5 *God is within her, she will not fall;*
God will help her at break of day.
6 *Nations are in uproar, kingdoms fall;*
he lifts his voice, the earth melts.
7 *The* LORD *Almighty is with us;*
the God of Jacob is our fortress. Selah

8 *Come and see the works of the* LORD,
the desolations he has brought on the earth.
9 *He makes wars cease to the ends of the earth;*
he breaks the bow and shatters the spear,
he burns the shields with fire.
10 *"Be still, and know that I am God;*
I will be exalted among the nations,
I will be exalted in the earth."

11 *The* LORD *Almighty is with us;*
the God of Jacob is our fortress. Selah

CHAPTER ELEVEN

WHEN YOUR STRESSES
ARE GREATER THAN YOUR STRENGTHS

A man went to his doctor complaining about severe headaches. He was told to stop smoking, which he did. The headaches persisted. Then he was told to stop using alcohol. He did, but the headaches continued. Finally, it was discovered that he was wearing a size-fifteen collar on a size-sixteen neck. That will certainly give anyone a headache!

Many things can cause headaches: defective vision, poor lighting, smog, tobacco smoke. Some headaches come from emotional problems. When people endure some degree of stress, the body produces adrenaline, a built-in protection system that makes more blood circulate in the brain. This in turn causes the brain to swell inside the skull—which does not swell. Pressure builds up and headaches are the result. Pain is the outcome, and that pain is a warning signal that your stress level is too high. So stress can cause headaches metaphorically and literally. Next time you say, "My teenage son is a real headache," you may well be hitting the nail on the head!

Some degree of stress is unavoidable in this world. In fact, stress is necessary if human beings are to function adequately. Many students need the stress of an examination to make them study; soldiers need the stress of a kit inspection to get themselves cleaned up; athletes respond to the stress of the big game. But overwhelming situations can produce stress that is more than some people can handle, unless they know the true source of strength.

HOW TO KNOW GOD INTIMATELY

"God is our refuge and strength, an ever-present help in trouble." (v. 1)

Consider the first verse of this psalm: *"God is our refuge and strength, an ever-present help in trouble."* Take note of the three things that God has shown to the teachable psalmist:

- He is a refuge.
- He is a strength.
- He is an ever-present help.

Realizing these things about God requires an acceptance of what the Bible teaches. This should be followed by a willingness to trust yourself to what you have accepted. Understanding that God is a refuge when you are under stress is the first step. But the second step is to communicate with him about the stress and seek his protection and preserving grace. He will act on your behalf and thereby show you another aspect of his being. You will become aware in a practical sense that he truly can be your *"refuge."* And accordingly, you will know him in a fuller way.

No doubt you have had the experience of discovering

that friends are sometimes absent in time of trouble. When all was going well, they were with you. But when things started to come apart at the seams, they suddenly became conspicuous by their absence. Such people may have a tough time coping with their own difficulties and, therefore, have no intention of getting involved in the troubles of others. Not so the Lord. He is *"an ever-present help in trouble."*

Down through the history of the church, there have been men and women who have proved this conclusively. When the Covenanters were being hauled across the glens by the English dragoons, they took great comfort from the psalms, not the least the one that assured them that the Lord was ever present. When Martin Luther was up to his ears in trouble with the pope, he rejoiced in God's presence and wrote his most famous hymn, "Ein Feste Burg Ist Unser Gott" ("A Mighty Fortress Is Our God") because of the inspiration of this psalm. It was in their moments of stress and distress that Luther and the Covenanters came to know the Lord in a deeper dimension. So does everyone who leans on the strength of the Lord.

DON'T FEAR STRESS

"Therefore we will not fear, though the earth give way and the mountains fall into the heart of the sea, though its waters roar and foam and the mountains quake with their surging." (vv. 2–3)

Thomas H. Holmes and his colleagues at the University of Washington have done considerable research into the subject of stress. They came to the conclusion that an accumulation of two hundred or more "life changing units" in any one year may mean more disruption than an individual can stand. On their scale, death of a spouse equals one hundred units, divorce equals seventy-three units, and the Christmas holidays equal twelve units!

The psalmist had no scale of life-change units to help him, but he had plenty of exposure to shattering experiences. In magnificent poetic language, he said that he would not fear *though the earth give way and the mountains fall into the heart of the sea, though its waters roar and foam and the mountains quake with their surging.* He certainly had his share of troubles.

He had known times of shaking in his life as though an earthquake had hit him. His had experienced crisis like a roaring, swamping flood. He had felt at times that the very rocks under his feet were moving. And so do many people I have known.

I remember preaching a message from this psalm titled "When Trouble Comes." The next day a woman called and said she was in the hospital. I went to see her immediately because the news she gave me was shattering. She had been sitting in church listening to my sermon and thinking how free from trouble she and her family had been. In fact, she told me that she vaguely wondered how she would react if and when real trouble came her way. She didn't have to wait long. On Monday she went for a routine medical checkup and was told she had leukemia.

But rather than panic, she reacted to her crisis in the way we will learn about in Psalm 46.

All of us will have to face stressful situations at some time or other, so it is very important that we prepare for them. Death, illness, separation, financial problems, business worries, in-laws all play their part. Some may be more like earthquakes than others, but they all can shake us to some degree.

THERE IS A RIVER

"There is a river whose streams make glad the city of God, the holy place where the Most High dwells. God is within her, she will not fall; God will help her at break of day."
(vv. 4–5)

This psalm quite possibly was written to be sung by choirs after a great victory over enemies who threatened Jerusalem. To the people in the surrounding city, the warfare had seemed like earthquakes and floods and total disaster. But now the warfare is over and the celebrating begins.

"There is a river whose streams make glad the city of God," and *"God is within her."* The picture of a river in the middle of the city is very beautiful in this context. Sieges can be withstood a lot better when there is a river in the besieged city! Whatever the actual circumstances of the writing of the psalm may have been, there is no doubt that the real river to which the psalmist refers is the Lord himself. He is the river flowing to the aid of people under pressure. It is he who

provides life-giving water to those who are surrounded by severe testings and trauma.

Franz Delitzsch, the renowned Old Testament scholar, sees a parallel between these thoughts and Isaiah's beautiful words: "There the LORD will be our Mighty One. It will be like a place of broad rivers and streams. No galley with oars will ride them, no mighty ship will sail them" (Isaiah 33:21). What an encouragement these words are to those in the midst of shock, who can take them to heart and discover the reality of the indwelling Lord in their lives and the cool, peaceful flow of his water of life in their souls.

FROM HEAD TO HEART

"The LORD Almighty is with us; the God of Jacob
is our fortress." (v. 7)

If it is true that God is a refuge (v. 1), it must be equally true that those who move into him have nothing to fear. So they can say with assurance, "Therefore we will not fear, though the earth give way" (v. 2). If it is true that the Lord is within the holy city, then it must be equally true that the city of God "will not fall" (v. 5). And no matter what we face, we are not alone, "the Lord Almighty is with us."

These facts are true. Moving from the stage of accepting the facts of scriptural truth is a giant step for us. Getting theology from head to heart, so that it affects the flow of blood from heart to head, is the key to dealing with much of the emotional stress to which we are all subjected.

I have often told people that the pressures of the pastorate are so immense that, without an adequate working theology, I would doubt my ability to survive. By "working theology" I mean a belief that really believes, a faith that really expects, and a trust that really anticipates. It is an awesome task to stand in front of a congregation week after week, knowing that you are God's spokesperson. When I stand in the pulpit, I know there are hundreds of people, thousands of sins, scores of needs, dozens of misunderstandings sitting there waiting in people with a host of different attitudes; and one fallible person is expected to stand before them and say, "Thus says the Lord . . ." I have been in many stressful situations, but none equals that kind of stress.

My phone rings, and a stranger at the other end of the line says, "My mother has had a stroke and is partially paralyzed. She has pneumonia and needs antibiotics. The rest of my family says we should withhold the medication and let her die peacefully, but I don't know. What do you think I should do?"

This is stress. But do you know something? I sleep well at night! The reason is this: I have discovered over the years that the Lord indwells me by his Spirit. He is my strength, my stronghold, and my sufficiency. Constantly, I have to respond to the stress situations in which I find myself by relaxing in the Lord and responding to what I know of him. For instance, when I have spent hours in personal and sermon preparation, I stand before the people breathing a verse of a hymn ("O for a Thousand Tongues to Sing") by John Wesley in prayer:

> My gracious Master and my God
> Assist me to proclaim
> To spread through all the earth abroad
> The honors of Thy name.

God answers that prayer and I feel the stress leave. Fully relaxed in anticipation of his blessing, I preach my heart out! Another hymn, "Dear Lord and Father of Mankind," with words by John Greenleaf Whittier, that is continually in my thinking and praying when I am under stress is:

> Drop Thy still dews of quietness
> Till all our strivings cease
> Take from our souls the strain and stress
> And let our ordered lives confess
> The beauty of Thy peace.

REVIEW FOR A NEW VIEW

"Come and see the works of the Lord. . . ." (v. 8a)

There is a kind of reminiscence that is unhealthy. Paul knew this and said, "Forgetting what is behind and straining toward what is ahead, I press on toward the goal" (Philippians 3:13–14).

"History is bunk," said automobile tycoon Henry Ford. It

is a "dust heap" in the eyes of Augustine Birrell. German philosopher Georg Wilhelm Hegel expressed similar if more cultured sentiments: "What experience and history teach is this—that people and governments never have learned anything from history or acted on principles deduced from it."

Ford, Birrell, and Hegel notwithstanding, we must insist that the history of God's dealings with people is of immense value to those living under stress. Periodic review of what he has done is a vital necessity. As the psalmist says, "*Come and see the works of the LORD.*" In its historical context, this call had to do with the Lord's intervention in the affairs of his people as he delivered Jerusalem from her enemies. But it is perfectly legitimate for us to take it as an invitation to review what God has done down through the centuries. Read about the many occasions in Old Testament times when God showed himself ready and willing to "strengthen those whose hearts are fully committed to him" (2 Chronicles 16:9). Review the things that the Holy Spirit recorded concerning God's actions in the life of our Lord Jesus, in particular the "mighty strength, which he displayed in Christ when he raised him from the dead" (see Ephesians 1:19–20).

Then read through the Acts of the Apostles and enjoy learning about the things God did in establishing and building his church despite seemingly insurmountable odds. Add to this a steady diet of missionary biographies. As you read, revel in the fact that the God of Isaac and Jacob, David and Jonathan, Paul and Silas, Luther and Wesley is your God too. That'll help the stress to go.

THE VALUE OF BEING STILL AND KNOWING GOD
"Be still, and know that I am God. . . ." (v. 10)

It seems strange that the Lord should tell people confronted with earthquakes and floods and assorted disasters to do exactly the opposite of what their instincts tell them to do. "Run," says instinct. "Be still," says the Lord. I'm not suggesting that in a literal flood you should be still or that in an earthquake you should not take evasive action. But I do believe that when the troubles of life overtake us we should, instead of running away from them in hysteria, take time to be still. The full statement is "Be still, and know that I am God."

It is not too difficult to be cool, calm, and collected when there is nothing to give you a headache. Composure is relatively simple when there is nothing to "push you over the edge." But to be able to react to the unexpected in this unnatural way is difficult. So far as I know, there is only one way of doing it. That is to be so accustomed to being still in the Lord's presence that it becomes an intuitive reaction.

A well-trained soldier will freeze instantly if he hears some sound that he is not expecting. It takes long hours of training to enable him to freeze quickly enough to save his life. That's how it is with the one who would be still in the Lord when the unexpected happens. I am sure that the woman who was diagnosed with leukemia was able to respond to her earthquake as calmly as she did because she had spent considerable time learning of the Lord and his ways prior to going into the hospital. People do various things when they are being still. Some spend that time focusing on themselves and their problems. Others ponder mysterious questions such as "What is the sound of one hand clapping?" Some silently meditate on pyramids. Others stand on their heads. But the psalmist gives explicit instructions to people learning stillness: They are to stop and *"know that I am God."*

To *"know"* can mean different things. Ask people in the street if they know the president of the United States, and most will say yes. That does not mean that they know the president personally; most of them probably have never seen him in person. It means only that they know who the president is.

To be acquainted with who God is may be a start, but it is nothing more. To know him in an intimate, personal way is what is needed. In the Old Testament the verb *to know* meant such intimacy of relationship that it was often used to describe the sexual activity between husband and wife. It is important that we understand the depth of meaning used here. We are to take time and get to know God deeply.

SPECIAL ATTENTION
"Selah." (v. 11b)

The little word *Selah* (vv. 3, 7, 11) occurs seventy-one times in the book of Psalms. It is rather ironic that, while it is so common, no one is quite sure what it means. Some think it was a musical sign that gave instructions to the singers and instrumentalists. Others feel that it had liturgical significance and signaled the point in public worship where the congregation should respond.

Whatever the full meaning of the term, it is obvious that it was used to draw special attention to what had just been said. This special attention might come through a musical "forte," through a liturgical prostrating or uplifting of the hands and eyes, or even through a rip-roaring "Hallelujah!" The point surely is that the things of God as presented in psalms like this will have great bearing on our lives—if we will give special attention to what has been said.

Be still, therefore. Give yourself time to know God. Respond to what you know. Review what he has done and relate him to your stress. Then see his peace reign in your heart.

Psalm 51

¹ *Have mercy on me, O God,*
according to your unfailing love;
according to your great compassion
blot out my transgressions.
² *Wash away all my iniquity*
and cleanse me from my sin.

³ *For I know my transgressions,*
and my sin is always before me.
⁴ *Against you, you only, have I sinned*
and done what is evil in your sight,
so that you are proved right when you speak
and justified when you judge.

....

⁷ *Cleanse me with hyssop, and I will be clean;*
wash me, and I will be whiter than snow. . . .

....

⁹*Hide your face from my sins*
and blot out all my iniquity.

¹⁰ *Create in me a pure heart, O God,*
and renew a steadfast spirit within me.
¹¹ *Do not cast me from your presence*
or take your Holy Spirit from me.
¹² *Restore to me the joy of your salvation*
and grant me a willing spirit, to sustain me.

¹³ *Then I will teach transgressors your ways,*
and sinners will turn back to you.
¹⁴ *Save me from bloodguilt, O God,*
the God who saves me,
and my tongue will sing of your righteousness.
¹⁵ *O Lord, open my lips,*

and my mouth will declare your praise.
16 *You do not delight in sacrifice, or I would bring it;*
you do not take pleasure in burnt offerings.
17 *The sacrifices of God are a broken spirit;*
a broken and a contrite heart,
O God, you will not despise.

18 *In your good pleasure make Zion prosper;*
build up the walls of Jerusalem.
19 *Then there will be righteous sacrifices,*
whole burnt offerings to delight you;
then bulls will be offered on your altar.

CHAPTER TWELVE

WHEN YOU FEEL
LIKE A TOTAL FAILURE

In a society where success is the name of the game, it's hard to be a failure. When outer trappings of wealth and power mean you are a winner, then those with less often feel like losers. When everybody loves a winner, losers are lonely people. But there is hope!

GOD LOVES FAILURES

It ought to be obvious that the only way for one person to become a competitive winner is for another person to be a loser. Therefore, there have to be as many losers as winners around. The problem is knowing a loser when we see one. We set up our standards of success, establish our own criteria, and merrily evaluate one another. But the awful thought that hits some of us is that the criteria we have chosen so arbitrarily may be faulty. Faulty criteria produce faulty evaluations.

God refuses to be terribly impressed with dollars earned and honors gained. He has difficulty seeing the ultimate value in the number of "first places" gained or goals achieved. But we humans are still impressed by

such criteria, and we insist on evaluating personal success by them.

God, however, has other standards that he has consistently used from the beginning, and we should carefully consider these criteria for evaluating personal worth. It takes little study of these standards to realize the extent to which all people have failed. But while God makes no bones about being displeased by human failure, he makes it abundantly clear that he has great love and concern for those who have failed.

YOU'RE IN GOOD COMPANY

Some years ago I preached a message about John Mark, the young man who went with Paul and Barnabas on a missionary journey, got cold feet, and deserted them. This young man eventually became the author of the second gospel—a striking story of God not only loving a failure but being willing to use a failure. At the end of the service, a young man who had been participating in the program came to me and said, "I have been in Christian work for years, but this is the first time I have heard that God loves and uses failures. I work in a situation where we have a constant stream of successful businessmen, athletes, movie stars, and political figures giving testimony to their faith in Christ. I got the impression there must be something seriously wrong with me because I am such a failure, and they all seem like colossal successes."

It was my joy to spend long hours with that young

man showing him the history book of Scripture and the way it faithfully records the failures of its heroes. Noah got drunk. Moses got angry. Gideon got scared. Peter could be inconsistent. Paul was inconsiderate. Thomas doubted. Martha pouted. But God dealt with them and used every one of them for his glory and for our blessing.

KING-SIZE FAILURE

David the king, however, is one whose monumental failure is described in detail, not for our titillation but for our edification. In addition to its historical description of David's failure (2 Samuel 11–12), Scripture is careful to record David's own account of his steps back from failure. Psalm 51, one of my favorite passages of inspired writing, gives us the details.

The psalm starts with great anguish of heart but ends with a great sense of worship and hope. The verses in between are full of truths that those who are conscious of failure should understand. Take time to read Psalm 51 now. As you read, notice that the key to David's comeback from the edge of disaster is the word *spirit*, which is used four times in the psalm:

- Renew a steadfast *spirit* within me (v. 10b).
- Do not . . . take your *Holy Spirit* from me (v. 11b).
- Grant me a willing *spirit*, to sustain me (v. 12b).
- The sacrifices of God are a broken *spirit* (v. 17a).

There was a spiritual cause for David's failure, so there had to be a spiritual answer. The same is true of most failure.

A Wrong Spirit

David's request for the renewal of a steadfast or "right" spirit (v. 10) was an admission that his actions had been motivated by a wrong spirit. This is further substantiated by his acknowledgment that, before God can bless and use anyone who has failed, that person must have a broken spirit (v. 17).

A brief look at the circumstances that led to the writing of this psalm will show clearly the nature of David's wrong spirit. Scripture records it this way: "In the spring, at the time when kings off to war, David sent Joab . . ." (2 Samuel 11:1). David stayed home while Joab and the rest of his troops went to war. A classic case of "Lord, here am I, send *him!*" The writer went on to explain, "One evening David got up from his bed" (v. 2). Now, the wrong spirit is very clearly exposed. It was a spirit of laziness! No red-blooded king stays in bed while his men are on the field of battle! The king had a case of the royal blahs. Wise old Isaac Watts had it right when he said:

In works of labor or of skill,
I would be busy too,
For Satan finds some mischief still
For idle hands to do.

That is exactly what happened to David. As he got up from his bed, he saw Bathsheba, beautifully posed on her rooftop across the street. At that point, David's wrong spirit took him over completely. David desired Bathsheba, he wanted her, he sent for her, and he had his way with her.

As a result of the illicit union, Bathsheba became pregnant. David found himself in a real fix because Uriah, her husband, was still away at war and therefore could not be assumed to have fathered his wife's child. David concocted a scheme for getting himself off the hook. He brought Uriah home on furlough and told him to take a few days off with his wife. But Uriah, out of respect for the men he had left behind on the battlefield, wouldn't allow himself the pleasure of being with his wife. David got him drunk, but Uriah still wouldn't go home to Bathsheba. He was a better drunk man than the king was sober! Adding one horrible sin to another, David then manipulated Uriah's battle assignment and in effect had him killed in action. David's sole interest was the saving of his own skin.

Confronted with Truth

God then sent the prophet Nathan on a very ticklish assignment: Nathan confronted the king by means of a story that had the king trapped before he realized its significance. He told David about a rich man who stole the only lamb of a poor neighbor. David boiled with rage and righteous indignation as he listened. *"You are the man,"* declared the intrepid Nathan (2 Samuel 12:7), and David broke into little pieces. He was suddenly overcome with a sense of his own guilt. Some people in similar circumstances react against God's messenger. This was not so with David. He accepted the exposure honestly and promptly took steps to deal with the situation.

REPENTANCE AND CLEANSING

"Have mercy on me, O God, according to your unfailing love; according to your great compassion blot out my transgressions. Wash away all my iniquity and cleanse me from my sin. . . . Cleanse me with hyssop, and I will be clean; wash me, and I will be whiter than snow." (vv. 1–2, 7)

Any comeback from failure necessitates an honest confrontation and adequate dealings with the sin committed. There is a terrible danger that we will condone the sin that God condemns. There is a possibility that we will cultivate the selfishness that God repudiates. But a person with a broken spirit is prepared to think as God thinks, and is prepared to call sin sin, and to deal with it the only way possible—with repentance and cleansing.

Coming to the point of repentance is often very hard. It is my opinion that it is made harder when we do not understand that it is the goodness of God that leads us to repentance (Romans 2:4 KJV). David knew this, for he talked of God's *"lovingkindness"* and *"tender mercies"* (v. 1 KJV). Obviously, he had a real sense of God's love and grace toward him. Not that he forgot that God deals in "truth in the inner parts" (v. 6) and insists on being "justified" when he judges (v. 4). But David was swamped by the thought of God still being prepared to love the one who does not deserve such love. This is the beauty of being a failure. God can't do much for successful people because they are so busy being complimented on their successes that they have little time for seeing themselves realistically. As a result, they feel little need for repentance. But failures have a great time being honest and realistic and loved and forgiven.

SPIRITUAL RENEWAL FOR FAILURES

"Create in me a pure heart, O God, and renew a steadfast spirit within me." (v. 10)

I remember the first time I was really confronted with the reality of my own failure. It was both excruciating and exhilarating. It was excruciating because out of my love for the Lord I wanted to serve him wholeheartedly; and yet the more I endeavored to serve him, the more I appeared to fail him. The more intimately I knew him, the more intimately I got to know myself. And my self-discovery was a disappointment, to put it mildly.

But it was also exhilarating because I realized that I was discovering what God had known all the time. And knowing the immensity of my failure had not altered God's attitude toward me one fraction. It seemed as if I had a new vision of the grace and wonder of God. He actually loved me as I was and intended to work with me as I was. Then and only then was I open to discover more of the resources that were mine in Christ. You could call my experience a "renewal of a steadfast spirit."

This new spirit began to change many things. God would have nothing to do with laziness. He wanted to see some discipline. He hated wantonness and looked for a giving spirit. Selfishness was in total opposition to everything God stood for, so that had to die. I found myself being made new and fresh within and without.

THE HOLY SPIRIT

"Do not cast me from your presence or take your Holy Spirit from me." (v. 11)

At this point we must make it quite clear that the steadfast and right spirit of which David speaks in this psalm is in essence the Holy Spirit—or at least the product of his indwelling and outworking. This is confirmed by the words *"do not . . . take your Holy Spirit from me."*

In the days of the Old Testament, the Holy Spirit would "come upon" people in order to equip them for specific tasks. He anointed prophets, priests, and kings for divine service. On occasion, if the anointed one failed in his service and showed little or no evidence of rectifying that which was wrong, the Holy Spirit would depart from him. This happened in the case of David's predecessor Saul (1 Samuel 16:14). But David need not have worried, for his own heart was open and warm to the Lord; and the Lord had no intention of withdrawing David from service.

In our days we have a fuller experience of the Holy Spirit. Since Pentecost, the prayer of the Lord Jesus has been fulfilled: "And I will ask the Father, and he will give you another Counselor to be with you forever" (John 14:16). This means that a believer can settle down to maintaining a broken spirit, in order that he or she may know the freshness and beauty of a right spirit. The degree to which a person can reject the old spirit will have a major bearing on the way in which he or she can be governed by the new spirit. Or as Paul put it, "If you live according to the sinful nature, you will die; but if by the Spirit you put to death the misdeeds of the body, you will live" (Romans 8:13).

FREEDOM FROM SELF-CENTEREDNESS AND SELF-TRUST

"Restore unto me the joy of thy salvation; and uphold me with thy free spirit." (v. 12 KJV)

A boy who had been learning something of the truths contained in this psalm said that he felt as though he had been holding his breath all his life, and now for the first time he could exhale. He was expressing something of the sentiments expressed in the phrase *"uphold me with thy free spirit."* It was a liberating experience for him. The word *free* in this context does not mean "without cost." Rather, it means "liberating." The work of the Spirit as he floods our lives is to uphold us in a liberating experience. He has no desire to see us permanently crippled by guilt or wretchedly broken and despairing.

Guilt when dealt with, brokenness when healed, despair when banished are preludes to the liberating peace and joy that only those motivated by the Spirit of God can experience.

There is liberty from self-centeredness. This is implied by the expression *"your salvation."* Most of the time we are so concerned about ourselves that we talk about "my salvation." It would appear that David was being very careful to acknowledge that even his salvation is the work of God. He couldn't take credit for being saved. What's more, he didn't want to take credit for anything. He was far too liberated for that kind of thing!

Watch yourself for a day or two and see how often you use the word *my* when *your/God's* would be much more appropriate. The beauty of being liberated from self-centeredness is that you hold everything in much higher regard. It's one thing to talk and think about *my* house, but it's much more challenging to regard it as *God's*, and use it accordingly. *My* time can be such a burden, but when it is *his*, the days and the hours become so much more rewarding and enriching. *My* money can be such a worry, but if it is *his*, it becomes a matter of glad stewardship rather than constant stewing.

In a society that teaches you to be your own person and do your own thing, it is increasingly difficult not to become deluded with a sense of self-sufficiency. To some extent it is necessary for people to have confidence in their God-given abilities, but deeply ingrained self-trust will lead to disaster.

In David's case, he was so open to temptation and so prone to wander that self-trust was a luxury he could no longer afford. So he prayed to be sustained, or "upheld," by God's Spirit. He did not think it unmasculine to admit weakness. He did not feel it demeaning to his kingly role to confess his total inadequacy.

So many people are not free to be honest about their failures. They must "save face" at all costs. They must, if they are British, "keep a stiff upper lip." This is no problem to the liberated failures, for they have nothing to hide and are free to be open about their needs and to be open to the One who is the only answer to those needs.

It is great good news that you don't have to trust your untrustworthy self, but instead you can trust the Lord who is faithful. And it is thrilling news to know that you can be free to admit your trust in God.

FREEDOM FROM SELF-INTEREST

"Then I will teach transgressors your ways, and sinners will turn back to you. . . . Then there will be righteous sacrifices, whole burnt offerings to delight you. . . ." (v. 13, 19)

I am always moved when I read David's proclamation here. The first thing that moves me is that this man so recently wounded and wounding had discovered such forgiveness, cleansing, and healing that he was free from his own troubles and eager to be of service to others. The second moving aspect of this verse is the fact that David spoke with great assurance: *"sinners will turn back to you."* There is no suggestion that he had taken his traumatic experience of failure lightly; it was simply that he was aware that failure is not final.

David also became preoccupied with the affairs of Zion and Jerusalem. His thoughts turned to the possibility of the Lord being *"delight[ed]"* with *"righteous sacrifices."* To be set free from the bondage of a spiritual concern that goes no further than the extent of your own need and to reach out to the spiritual needs of others is liberty indeed. To be free to consider the possibility of doing something that will bring delight to the Lord is exhilarating indeed.

FREEDOM FROM SELF-PITY

"Save me from bloodguilt, O God, the God who saves me, and my tongue will sing of your righteousness. . . . My mouth will declare your praise." (vv. 14–15b)

David had plenty of grounds for guilt. There was seemingly no sin too great for him to perpetrate. Yet he refused to be bound by guilt and self-pity. "Set me free from these things because of the depth of your forgiveness" is what he meant by *"Save me from bloodguilt."* He had no intention of keeping his mouth shut out of shame or of hiding the truth and pretending that everything had always been well. With the freedom that only the forgiven know, he determined in his heart to testify to the grace of God in his life. *"My tongue will sing of your righteousness. . . . My mouth will declare your praise."*

The person who lives in an aura of perpetual success and has to maintain that kind of image is in bondage to his or her own myth. The self-confessed failure, with the enabling, liberating Spirit driving him, has much more freedom and packs much more clout—because of the ring of reality in what the person says, does, and is. Strange as it may seem, the way to success is failure. So if you want to succeed, don't fail to fail.

GOD'S WAY WORKS

I trust that as we have studied these psalms together, you have discovered in them, as I have, a great reservoir of comfort and challenge. It is encouraging to realize that God's Word recognizes and addresses our inmost feelings, fears, and failings. It is good to know of the personal experience of the inspired writers who, perhaps to our surprise, experienced what we experience today and found answers in the Lord. But best of all, the psalms remind us of what works when life doesn't simply because God is still working in our lives for his good purposes. And it is God who makes life work.